"*Companions in Suffering* is an honest, clear, biblical, practical, and wise book, speaking to many of the issues we wrestle with most. If you are suffering, Wendy Alsup will be an open and encouraging companion."

Andrew Wilson, teaching pastor, King's Church London

"No one who is really suffering is interested in trite answers or simple formulas; we want something substantive. We want to hear from someone who has been there and is honest about the pain but offers genuine insight into what it looks like to persevere through the pain. That's what Wendy Alsup does in this book. While it's personal, it isn't personality-driven or all about her personal story, though her personal story gives her writing credibility. Instead, this book is saturated with insight into Scripture, presenting meaty truths that make a difference, helping to make sense of and bring peace and rest in the midst of the lowest days and the hardest things."

Nancy Guthrie, author and Bible teacher

"Shaped by a deep commitment refined in the crucible of loss and pain, Wendy Alsup writes about a subject few of us would choose to explore me point in our lives. *Companions in Suff* one with wide application as Alsup n und scrip- tural application. She doesn't offer ea richer: com- passion and companionship for those journeying o is suffering or for those walking through the valley of the shadow in th n lives."

Michelle Van Loon, author of *Born to Wander: Recovering the Value of our Pilgrim Identity*

"Few things are more isolating for a person than suffering, and that isolation only compounds the pain that suffering brings upon a person. Wendy Alsup understands this pain well and has given us all a gift in the midst of her suffering. Through her own narrative, the stories of others, and the testimony of Scripture, Wendy reminds us that we truly are never alone in our suffering. This book is a gift for anyone who is stuck in a deep valley, because Wendy understands that the valley doesn't always have an exit point. And instead of showing us the path out, she gives us the Christ within—the same Christ who has met her in her dark valley. Wendy has been a gift to me personally for a while now, and I am excited for others to experience that same comfort through her words."

Courtney Reissig, author of *Glory in the Ordinary: Why Your Work in the Home Matters to God* and *Teach Me to Feel: Worshiping God Through the Psalms in Every Season of Life*

"*Companions in Suffering* is filled with encouragement from a fellow companion who knows Christ and the power of His resurrection, because she has shared deeply in the fellowship of his suffering. This stewardship of her suffering offers the life-giving help and hope that only Christ can bring."

Karen Hodge, coordinator of women's ministries for the Presbyterian Church in America (PCA) and author of *Transformed: Life-Taker to Life-Giver and Life-Giving Leadership*

"Wendy welcomes us into her tent of suffering, encouraging us to enter into others' tents and welcome them into ours. She doesn't do so with empty platitudes or false promises but with the hope of the gospel and the truth of Scripture. In your own sufferings, be comforted by God through Wendy's witness."

Kristen Wetherell, author of *Fight Your Fears* and coauthor *of Hope When It Hurts*

"This is recommended reading. Here is a book filled with both exegesis and examples of pain and patience, of sorrow and rejoicing. Through the use of personal pictures and biblical reflections, Wendy Alsup offers all of us the way forward in the midst of suffering. There are no easy fixes here or trite comforts, but there is a steady stream of personal, sympathetic anecdotes and Christ-centered encouragements. Suffering can be lonesome, but Wendy reminds us that we never really suffer alone. Jesus Christ was a man of sorrows and thus sympathizes with our sorrows as well. If you or someone you know is suffering, allow Wendy to come alongside and help you see Jesus again."

Tony Carter, lead pastor of East Point Church, Atlanta

"Author Wendy Alsup has a gift for you. It's a refreshingly honest look at how hard life can be set against the backdrop of the gospel. She takes readers on a survey of the hurts of her own life and frames human pain with biblical hope."

Dan DeWitt, associate professor of applied theology and apologetics at Cedarville University, author of *Life in the Wild: Fighting for Faith in a Fallen World*

COMPANIONS
IN SUFFERING

COMFORT FOR TIMES OF
LOSS AND LONELINESS

———

WENDY ALSUP
FOREWORD BY TRILLIA J. NEWBELL

An imprint of InterVarsity Press
Downers Grove, Illinois

InterVarsity Press
P.O. Box 1400, Downers Grove, IL 60515-1426
ivpress.com
email@ivpress.com

InterVarsity Press® is the book-publishing division of InterVarsity Christian Fellowship/USA®, a movement of students and faculty active on campus at hundreds of universities, colleges, and schools of nursing in the United States of America, and a member movement of the International Fellowship of Evangelical Students. For information about local and regional activities, visit intervarsity.org.

Scripture quotations marked CSB have been taken from the Christian Standard Bible®, Copyright © 2017 by Holman Bible Publishers. Used by permission. Christian Standard Bible® and CSB® are federally registered trademarks of Holman Bible Publishers.

Published in association with the literary agent Don Gates of The Gates Group, www.the-gates-group.com.

While any stories in this book are true, some names and identifying information may have been changed to protect the privacy of individuals.

Cover design and image composite: David Fassett
Interior design: Jeanna Wiggins
Images: old grunge paper © paladin13 / iStock / Getty Images Plus
    watercolor © lutavia / iStock / Getty Images Plus
    colorful pedals © Halfdark / Getty Images
    gold foil texture © Katsumi Murouchi / Moment Collection / Getty Images
    red Rose © MirageC / Moment Collection / Getty Images
    postage stamp border © troyek / E+ / Getty Images

ISBN 978-0-8308-4586-6 (print)
ISBN 978-0-8308-4385-5 (digital)

Printed in the United States of America ∞

InterVarsity Press is committed to ecological stewardship and to the conservation of natural resources in all our operations. This book was printed using sustainably sourced paper.

Library of Congress Cataloging-in-Publication Data

A catalog record for this book is available from the Library of Congress.

P 25 24 23 22 21 20 19 18 17 16 15 14 13 12 11 10 9 8 7 6 5 4 3 2 1

Y 37 36 35 34 33 32 31 30 29 28 27 26 25 24 23 22 21 20

To Ellen,

who sat upright all night in the ICU

because nurses said you couldn't stay if you fell asleep,

listened to my angry and depressed ramblings over

multiple plates of sushi, took my kids to the fair

when I was too sick, and much more.

You have been God's hands and feet (and Uber driver)

again and again, a true companion for which

I and my family thank God.

CONTENTS

FOREWORD *by Trillia J. Newbell*   *ix*

1 On the Outside Looking In   *1*

2 Our Suffering Savior   *9*

3 Fellowship of the Suffering   *25*

4 Pleading for Rescue   *42*

5 Help My Unbelief   *56*

6 Ambiguous Loss   *73*

7 Learning to Lament   *85*

8 Finding Rest   *100*

9 Waiting on Jesus   *114*

10 Fellowship with the Cloud of Witnesses   *126*

11 Fellowship with the Rock   *139*

CONCLUSION: Limping Forward   *155*

ACKNOWLEDGMENTS   *161*

APPENDIX: Offering Companionship to the Suffering   *163*

NOTES   *173*

SUGGESTED READING   *177*

SCRIPTURE INDEX   *179*

FOREWORD

Trillia J. Newbell

After four miscarriages, the death of my father and oldest sister, and a recent surgery that required six weeks of rest, the Lord has allowed me ample opportunity to experience the loneliness of suffering.

For almost anyone, six weeks of semi-bed rest while also being conscious would be difficult. It was six weeks during the summer with two busy children and a long list of deadlines. What was I going to do? I never had the opportunity to become anxious because, before I knew it, friends were pouring in to help. I'm grateful beyond words for their swift care. I never said no to a single offer of help. From playdates for my kids to dinners for our dinner table, I said yes to it all.

But I haven't always been this way. I used to think I didn't need the gifts, time, and generosity of others. I had to grow in understanding my weakness and need. I needed to learn the beauty of humility. If the gospel is about receiving from Christ, why would I not want to also receive from others? As Wendy Alsup recounts in this book, at times we who suffer can withdraw, say no to those who love us, and alienate ourselves in our grief and pain. But learning to receive has been a gift not only for my own soul but also for those around me.

Whether you are like me and learning to receive from others, walking through a dark night of the soul, or holding up the head of your suffering friend, *Companions in Suffering* offers insight and wisdom that will help you.

The Bible has a great deal to say about giving and receiving. The church in Philippi, in particular, is a wonderful example for how our gifts affect others and, in their case, how their partnership in the gospel assisted the apostle Paul on his mission (Philippians 4:14-20).

Paul realized what a gift it was for others to be able to give. He wrote, "Not that I seek the gift, but I seek the profit that is increasing to your account" (Philippians 4:17). Paul had been well supplied by the Philippians, but it wasn't their gifts alone that he wanted to acknowledge. He wanted their character to be highlighted and credited—their generosity was evidence of spiritual maturity and growth (2 Corinthians 9:5). It was their gain to give even more than it was Paul's to receive their gift.

Similarly, when someone asks if they might be able to serve us, it is their gain to give. The giver has a chance to exercise humility, practice hospitality, or give generously. It also enables the giver to trust the Lord for their own provision (Philippians 4:19), just as we are trusting the Lord to provide for us. Recognizing the joy and blessing for the person who gives can help us receive when we are in our own dark, lonely places. Paul, who was suffering and in prison, wrote that he could do all things through Jesus who strengthened him (Philippians 4:13), but then he shared, "Still, you did well by partnering with me in my hardship" (v. 14). Paul was weak, he was needy, and he knew where to run. Paul ultimately needed God, but he realized God used people as an extension of his grace to Paul in his time of need.

If you, like me, felt strong before your season of suffering, you might be tempted to think you can or should be able to do it all on our own. You may be afraid to appear weak. Either way, we must preach truth to our hearts—when we are weak, then we are strong (2 Corinthians 12:9-11). We don't need to try to be the hero in our own story. God is the hero—we need only receive. And often God will use others as his hands and feet to provide exactly what we need. Receive from others, and as you do, you receive from the Lord.

Paul compares the gifts he received as "a fragrant offering" and a sacrifice acceptable and "pleasing to God" (Philippians 4:18). References such as a fragrant offering or pleasing aroma are drawn from the Old Testament (e.g., Genesis 8:21; Exodus 29:18). Their sacrifices were pleasing to God just as the generous gifts of the Philippian church were pleasing to the Lord. The ultimate sacrifice pleasing to the Lord was Jesus Christ. Jesus made a way so that we will never have to sacrifice again for our salvation.

The gospel is that we receive as a free gift eternal life through Jesus, who gave his life for us. When we give cheerfully and generously, it is a reflection of that ultimate gift and is pleasing to the Lord. And consequently we simply receive this free gift given by God. What an amazing exchange! As we give and receive, we are reflecting the gospel, which is all about the work of Jesus, who gave his life for us so we might receive eternal life.

In the words that follow, Wendy writes with vulnerability and wisdom of how we can receive spiritual refreshment through others and God's Word. She helps us find the companions God has given to walk with us through the long, dark night of the soul. Wendy takes us through the Scriptures to help us see that God has given us help, gifts, and companions to carry us through our suffering, including companions found right in the pages of Scripture. If you, like me, need to learn to receive from others, are walking through a long season of suffering, or are holding the hand of a suffering friend, *Companions in Suffering* will be a good companion for you.

ON THE OUTSIDE
LOOKING IN

"It's not catching."

A dear friend spoke these words to me over dinner as she lamented a divorce she did not want that had torn apart her life. She had first heard the phrase from another friend who was a widow after her husband died of cancer. Both expressed feeling like an outcast, a pariah, among former friends. Though friends initially endured with her widowed friend, over time her suffering seemed to mark her as *other*.

Those around her seemed unsure, even afraid of her, like her suffering would rub off on them and bring their lives down. But widowhood and even unwanted divorce are not communicable diseases. Despite that fact, the alienation felt by those who have gone through either is real. Sufferers often feel on the outside, looking in at the happy people they know enjoying the normal ups and downs of life.

I sat across the table from my friend, talking of her pain and loneliness, not realizing how quickly I would be overcome by my own. But soon I too would feel the same—like an outcast in the cold, watching through a window all the happy people enjoying each other's company around a warm, cozy fire. It is the worst kind of lonely feeling.

MY STORY

I grew up in Bible-teaching churches, and my parents were faithful to see I was in church every Sunday. Along the way I developed a sincere faith in Christ. But at some point during my teenage years, I learned in youth group what I now call the "Prosperity Gospel of Conservative Evangelicals."

Among churches that strongly condemned the health, wealth, and prosperity movement characterized by televangelists, I found a more subtle prosperity gospel can still quietly infiltrate the minds of immature believers. Though lots of people around me were suffering (if I looked hard enough to see them), I wrote off their suffering with some reason from their past. I assumed that perhaps their parents or they themselves had made poor choices at some crucial turn in life. Now, that mindset toward others seems quite immature and offensive.

My faithful Christian parents sent me to private school to protect me from perceived bad influences that would lead to instability. They were setting me up for a good life, so I thought. The underlying assumption in my youth and college years among youth leaders and my peers at Christian college was that if I (1) went to Bible college, (2) made wise choices while dating, and (3) generally sought God's will for my life, then I would have the foundation for a good, stable life serving God. I would be in the warm house with other happy Christians around the warm fire of God's love and Christian fellowship. That warm, cozy experience would be the natural result of making wise choices in my youth, or so I thought. I experienced this subtle but very real teaching at many points in multiple ministries well into adulthood.

But in my thirties that idea took a serious hit after church conflict tore apart the ministry I thought God had called me to. Things continued a slow downward spiral over the next few years, new trials added to old while few of the previous trials resolved. In particular, in my forties I walked a painful road in my marriage resulting in a divorce that I did not want. After I moved closer home to help my aging parents and receive their help as a single parent to my boys, I was diagnosed with breast cancer. A few months later, a CT scan found a large mass in my abdomen, and a few months later precancerous cells were discovered in my uterus. Multiple painful surgeries followed.

How could I raise my children or help my parents in my own ongoing medical crisis?

Didn't God know I needed to be strong for others?

Didn't God know that, as a single mom, my children and I didn't have the safety net for physical turmoil on top of relational problems?

What had I done to bring this all on myself? Why had God turned away from me?

As trial piled upon trial, my understanding of my place in God's kingdom was seriously challenged. I fought to get out of crisis mode, unable to envision my part in the body of Christ in such a state. I wanted to minister to others. I wanted to serve God through teaching or writing, through Bible studies in my home and outreach activities in my community. Instead, I was consumed by doctors' appointments and relational crises. I felt swallowed by the storm, drowning in the depths of stress and sorrow. Joy and happiness seemed forever out of my reach.

PARIAHS

At the most intense moments of my suffering, the only joy around me was the one just beyond my reach, among those whose suffering had let up. I stared at them as through a foggy window, praising God for the reconciliation of their struggle while I sat outside freezing in the cold, wondering how to reenter their warmth. When my suffering didn't let up and the things I hoped in dissolved, leaving me in the same or worse circumstances, I did not naturally say as the apostle Paul did in his letter to Corinth that I was overflowing with joy in all of my afflictions. As my own struggle endured, *I could only see the happiness of those around me who weren't suffering the same way.* Others seemed to flourish. Their relationships seemed happy, their bank accounts secure. They seemed healthy with happy children and secure homes. Their social media accounts showed happy families on happy vacations with happy friends.

By contrast, I felt like a pariah, on the outside looking in. Derived from a Tamil word for those kept from joining the drum line of a religious ceremony, the word *pariah* indicates one who is an outcast, dehumanized by their suffering and low status in the caste system of India.[1]

The friend I mentioned in the opening paragraph, whose husband left her after an emotional affair with a coworker in Christian ministry, drew my attention to this alienation sufferers can feel, like pariahs with a communicable disease. For unknown reasons, perhaps irrational fear that it might happen to their marriages as well, her friends distanced themselves, her circumstances challenging their own expectations and hopes of how their lives would turn out should they get too close to her.

Have you felt cast out by your circumstances, looking through a window at others enjoying life, whether at work, at church, or in your neighborhood? You can see their joy through the glass between you, but they don't seem to see your pain on the other side. Or maybe they see you on the outside but seem to back slightly away from the window in fear that your pain will seep into their lives. They politely distance themselves as if from one with a communicable disease that they are not vaccinated for.

I felt cast out by my own life circumstances—first as I walked into church weekly to sit in the pew on the row that our family of four had usually sat. Now we were only three, obviously missing a vital member of our family. While other families grew, mine shrank. Weekly I was confronted with that difference between me and those my family had previously fellowshiped with.

I felt other.

After I moved home and was diagnosed with cancer, this feeling of being on the outside looking in descended on me again. Though I didn't need chemotherapy for my breast cancer, I wore down as I recovered from one major surgery just to discover I needed another. And then another.

I missed one Sunday, two Sundays, then three, four, and a half dozen more over a nine-month period. I realized, like it or not, that our Sunday sermon series, Sunday school lessons, and women's group in my church, which I had previously been an integral part of, all went on without me.

This wasn't an evil conspiracy on the part of my church family but a simple fact of life. I could not blame folks for moving on with their lives. The churches I attended on both coasts were full of lovely people who sincerely cared for me physically and spiritually. But neither could I ignore the alienation I felt as I was left behind while they moved on with the normal rhythm of church life. Whether from medical necessity or broken relationships, feelings of alienation in the midst of a long season of suffering are quite normal, and they can have devastating consequences for our emotional well-being.

I have felt such alienation in the midst of pain quite often. Looking back at those times, though, I recognize that my feelings didn't reflect the truth among those in my church and community, and the rest of this book will reinforce the real ways we find community in suffering with others in the body of Christ, living and dead. But for a long season that feeling of alienation endured. I felt outside. I felt other, an orphan left on my own to navigate a path I didn't understand.

ATTACHMENT DISORDER IN THE BODY OF CHRIST

I have heard sad anecdotes about babies neglected in orphanages who have learned not to cry when they have a need because no one will come to help them. They ran out of tears, but their needs were still there. They often develop attachment disorders that make it extremely hard for them to attach to adoptive families when the time comes. I have at times found myself feeling weariness and detachment in my own long story of suffering. Why cry? Why call out to friends for help? And more devastating to consider, why pray?

I found there comes a point in our journeys when the tears cease, not because circumstances got better or the weight on our shoulders lightened, but simply because we are dehydrated. We don't have any tears left, and the weights on us keep us from even lifting our heads to see where we are in our journeys. Detaching from dark emotions seems the only way to survive. Yet how can we survive if we detach from God, his body, and his Word?

It is likely that you are reading this because you are carrying the heavy weight of suffering on your shoulders or love someone else who is. Maybe the weight is in the form of an unrelenting illness. Maybe it is the loss of a loved one in death or a broken relationship that you cannot mend on your own. Each of these is a heavy weight of suffering that seems to alienate us from others. Some find excuses for not being around us because deep in their psyche they perceive suffering as a communicable disease they don't want to catch. But sufferers often alienate themselves as well.

This book is for anyone enduring a long marathon of suffering who despairs of finding help or hope again. This book is for folks who don't cry anymore because their emotions are spent. And this book is for those persevering with their suffering loved ones. It can be as emotionally draining to watch a loved one suffer as to experience the suffering directly yourself.

If you have run out of tears and feel alone in your ongoing grief, if you are so weary from crying you feel detached from your emotions, God has not left you as an orphan. You have companions on this journey, first and foremost with Christ himself. But there is also companionship with his body, your brothers and sisters in the faith. We find companions among brothers and sisters still living and among those who have gone on before us. Finally, there is companionship and fellowship found in the words of Scripture, preserved eternally for us for our instruction, our comfort, and even our tears.

Come sit with me for a while in the pages of this book. In the midst of the alienation and detachment that long seasons of suffering can cause, may you too find deep community as I have with Christ, his Word preserved eternally for us, and fellow believers who encourage us with their testimonies of suffering, endurance, and hope. You need these varied avenues to community desperately, as each gives different resources that help you to persevere. God hasn't left you alone to find these resources on your own.

Jesus promises in John 14:18, "I will not leave you as orphans, I am coming to you."

REFLECT

At the end of each chapter you'll find a set of questions. They are designed for personal reflection, but you are also invited to discuss them with a friend or a small group.

At the most intense points of suffering, we are often surrounded by family and friends. But as time goes on, feelings of loneliness, being on the outside looking in, can invade more and more. How have you felt being an outcast because of the weight of your particular suffering?

In what ways are these feelings based on your physical reality (for instance, being separated from friends or church while you undergo chemotherapy)?

In what ways do these feelings stem from your own inner grief (such as feeling alienated from friends with children after you have lost one of your own)?

Jesus told his disciples in John 14:18 that he would not leave them as orphans. He would not leave them fatherless and motherless. He would not leave them bereft of guidance, comfort, and support. Have you felt like an orphan as you navigate your long road of suffering?

In John 14:16 Jesus promises that God will send the Holy Spirit. How does Jesus' promise to his disciples of this Counselor (or Comforter) in John 14 apply to you as you navigate the road before you?

OUR SUFFERING SAVIOR

"Jesus wept."

John 11:35, in the middle of the story of Lazarus's resurrection, is the shortest verse in the Bible.

The verse markings in our modern Bibles weren't added until around the sixteenth century, and the average verse in the Bible is around twenty-five words in length. Why, then, did a French printer in the sixteenth century single out this particular verse to have only two words? Perhaps because they are noteworthy words. Perhaps these words struck that Frenchman as he prepared his Greek New Testament for printing. These words strike me too. Jesus, the Son of God who claimed to be one with the Father in heaven, *wept*. Our sovereign Lord, Creator of the world, *cried*.

When I read these words in John 11:35, I can't help but notice the context. Jesus is about to raise to life his friend Lazarus, who had died just days before. In fact, this chapter indicates that Jesus deliberately waited until Lazarus died to return to his friend. Jesus planned to do more than heal him from his sickness, which he had done for others many times before. He planned to show his authority over death itself! Jesus was about to resolve everyone's sorrow in the biggest way possible that day. Yet, when faced with the grief of those around him, Jesus wept. He felt the pain of those around him and mourned with them.

Jesus knew he was going to heal Lazarus. He knew he was about to put things right for that little family. We too who believe in Jesus' name have faith that he will make right every hard circumstance in our life. In this life or the next, I have full confidence that God will redeem and restore all things. That he will heal all sickness. That he will right all wrongs. That he will restore all that is broken. Still, Jesus wept. And I do too.

LONGING TO BE FREE

Both my divorce and my physical burdens have felt like heavy crosses. They weigh me down and cause me to mourn. That weighted feeling makes sense because they have each resulted in new burdens in my life, new responsibilities I didn't previously have. I have bills to pay that I did not have to pay before. I have ongoing physical problems that require ongoing surgeries, medicines, and adjustments to life that I did not have just a few years ago.

One of my greatest joys has been to teach the Bible to others. After I moved to the East Coast, I began leading a weekly women's Bible study at my church, often hosting in my home. Our last study was through the book of Joshua. We worked through a simple but profound study of the book by Kathleen Nielsen, as our pastor preached through Joshua in our Sunday sermon series. It was the best group study I had ever experienced. Scripture felt alive; the story of the battle for Jericho became relevant to our lives in the twenty-first century. The fellowship among us as we grew in our understanding of Scripture was sweet and deep.

Then I was diagnosed with cancer. Each time I thought I had recovered enough to participate again, I found out I needed another surgery. After a while, the other ladies in my church picked up with the study, as they should, without me. These ladies include some of the most precious sisters who have walked with me through my sickness. They sought to include me, but I simply didn't have the physical bandwidth to participate. As they began studying again without me, I inevitably felt on the outside, looking in. Though we all have the best of intentions for it not to happen, it seems virtually impossible for long-term sufferers to avoid the weight that feelings of alienation add to your already heavy load.

The hardest weight I have had to bear, though, has been the weight of new painful emotions in my children that have followed my divorce, our move across country, and my health issues. Those form a weight from which I can't free them or me. My boys have wept with pain I cannot ease. The only thing I can offer as a parent is to hold them and weep with them. I have longed for my boys and me to be free of these weights of suffering. All together the confluence of emotional, physical, and financial weights have seemed a barrier to the abundant life in Christ, to serving God and loving my neighbor.

"Then he said to them all, 'If anyone wants to follow after me, let him deny himself, take up his cross daily, and follow me'" (Luke 9:23).

In Luke 9 (and in Matthew 10:38-39 and Luke 14: 27), Jesus didn't instruct his disciples to shake off the weight of their crosses in order to better serve him. Instead, he said to take up the weight and follow him anyway. Jesus invited his disciples to follow him, weights of suffering and all. And the rest of the New Testament presents suffering not as a rare event a few believers will experience but as the Christian norm as we live in faith in a world sorely affected by the fall.

You could argue that suffering is a communicable disease after all, but one we've all caught from Adam at the fall. We all will have weights on our shoulders, and many have severely heavy crosses to carry. My cross has felt much heavier than I could personally bear because it is. But Jesus said, "Take it up, and follow me." This sounds hard, even a little unsympathetic on the part of Jesus. I don't want to take up these new weights in my life and follow Jesus anyway. I want God to relieve me of these weights! But if we look closer at Scripture, we see that God empathizes with us well, and though I'd rather him remove the weights altogether, he offers instead to carry these weights with me, even for me. *He does not leave us as orphans to carry the weight of suffering alone.*

MAN OF SORROWS

In Isaiah 53, the prophet taught that the coming Messiah would be well-acquainted with grief. He would be a "man of sorrows" (KJV). The Hebrew word translated *acquainted* is more often translated *knew* or *know*.[1] The Messiah would know grief. Our Savior would be familiar with the pain of our fallen world in a very personal way.

We too are well-acquainted with grief. You, like me, likely know pain in a very personal way. For those of us who have met grief in a personal way and become well-acquainted with the various trappings that come with it, being around others who have not met grief personally can be incredibly frustrating. You, like me, may feel alienated, choosing long, lonely walks rather than talking on the phone. Maybe you stare out the window by yourself in the dark of your room rather than joining conversations with others elsewhere.

My suffering has changed my personality from extroverted to introverted, from ENFJ to INFJ, using a Myers-Briggs Type Indicator. When my mind is clouded by the fog of suffering, being around others who seem oblivious and are not well-acquainted with grief only adds to my frustration as I sit face to face with my own.

But Jesus told his disciples poignantly before his death, "I will not leave you as orphans" (John 14:18). The miracle promise to all sufferers who believe in Christ is that we are, in fact, not alone. God himself dwells in us, with us. Furthermore, this one who accompanies us in our sorrow understands sorrow too, better even than we do. He is anything but oblivious to the trappings of suffering. Whatever depths of grief we bear, he has born up under more. We are indwelt by God the Spirit, who connects us to Jesus. He sits with us in the dark when we cannot bear to be around others. He paces with us when we cannot be still. He groans with us when we cannot put words to our own suffering (Romans 8:26).

Jesus has endured grief even greater than ours, yet the wealth of grief he has endured does not result in him minimizing ours. The author of Hebrews observes, "We do not have a high priest who is unable to sympathize with our weaknesses, but one who has been tempted in every way as we are, yet without sin" (Hebrews 4:15).

Jesus sympathizes with our weaknesses, meaning that he is "affected with the same feeling" that we feel.[2] In contrast to simple pity or feeling bad for another as someone on the inside looking out at one who is suffering, Jesus feels the same emotions *as the sufferer*. He feels the loneliness, the ache, the frustration, and the grief we do. Though he is God and never sinned in his grief, he walks with us with knowledge and understanding of exactly the struggles we face.

NOURISHMENT AT HIS TABLE

As noteworthy as it is to contemplate Jesus walking with us in an understanding way, the author of Hebrews teaches us another thing that the man of sorrows offers fellow sufferers. "Since he himself has suffered when he was tempted, he is able to help those who are tempted" (Hebrews 2:18).

I love to read this verse in the King James Version because it gives me insight into the depth of help that Jesus offers us: "In that he himself hath suffered being tempted, he is able to succour them that are tempted."

The Old English word *succour* alludes to the kind of life-giving nourishment a mother offers a newborn. Because Jesus well understands the grief and pressure we bear when suffering, he is able to nourish us in the temptations that go along with suffering (and the suffering that goes along with temptations). Isaiah teaches that Jesus bears our sicknesses and carries our pain (Isaiah 53:4). This man of sorrows who is well-acquainted with grief doesn't just offer us pep talks. He takes on himself the burdens we experience from the fall and carries them with, even for, us. In Luke 9, Jesus told his disciples to take up their cross and follow him. But Scripture teaches us that he bears this cross with and for us, for we could never carry it on our own.

In theological terms we are talking about our union with Christ. If we have faith in Jesus as our Savior, we are said then to be *in him* (see Colossians 2:6-7). Jesus speaks of himself as the vine and we as the branches (John 15:5). Paul says Jesus is the head, and we are his body (Ephesians 5:23). These pictures reflect our union with Christ, and the Holy Spirit is called the seal, deposit, and guarantee of this union (Ephesians 1:14). Because God has deposited the Holy Spirit to live within us, he literally has not left us alone as orphans as we wait on the fulfillment of all of his promises to us. From this very real connection we have with God, we find the nourishment to bear fruit as followers of Jesus even as we endure the worst that life on earth offers. From this union we find the supernatural strength beyond our own to bear up under the weight on us and follow Jesus anyway.

TAKEN HOLD BY CHRIST

In Philippians 3:10, Paul uses intriguing language when talking about his union with Christ: "My goal is to know him and the power of his resurrection and the fellowship of his sufferings, being conformed to his death." Paul goes on to say two verses later, "Not that I have already reached the goal or am already perfect, but I make every effort to take hold of it because I also have been taken hold of by Christ Jesus" (v. 12). Paul mixed active and passive language. Christ had taken hold of Paul, and Paul had a goal of taking hold of Christ back, of knowing Christ as Christ knew him. Like one riding in on a horse to pluck up a child caught in a disaster, Jesus Christ pulled Paul up and out of his unbelieving life. Christ held Paul tightly and was not letting go. But Paul didn't want to flail loosely in Jesus' arms. He wanted to take hold of the one who had taken hold of him. This would come from intimately knowing Christ and his suffering.

At each new turn in my journey of suffering, I have flailed, kicking and screaming in protest. Sometimes I have felt in free fall. Other times, particularly around my divorce, I felt my home was turning upside down with me tumbling around inside of it without anything solid to catch my fall. In such moments, I am slowly learning, like Paul, to envision myself turning into Jesus' arms, taking hold of him as he has hold of me. I know now that his love will not let me go, but I do not want to flail kicking and screaming in his arms as he holds me securely. I want to know Jesus the way he knows me.

How much better the ride is when we turn toward Jesus in his embrace and embrace him in return. Jesus wasn't letting Paul go. But Paul longed to actively participate in this good work Jesus was doing in and through him. I need to as well.

Paul wanted to know this one who plucked him out of the miry pit, to know the power of his resurrection and the fellowship of his sufferings, being conformed to his death. That last phrase is stark for those of us enduring long seasons of suffering. Again and again, I want relief from my suffering in this life. Temporary relief through a restored relationship or a disease that responds to treatment can be possible in this life. Yet, even if we find temporary relief from the suffering that weighs us down, ultimately, all of us are going to die. Paul, while writing this letter, was sitting in a prison cell and would die an early death a few years later. Death might be postponed, but until Jesus returns, it won't be delayed forever for any of us.

Turning in Jesus' arms to hold him as he held Paul, Paul desired to be conformed to Jesus even in death. It is a worthy goal—to understand death as Jesus did, to die with the same perspective that Jesus had. What perspective did Jesus have on his suffering and death? "For the joy that lay before him, he endured the cross, despising the shame, and sat down at the right hand of the throne of God" (Hebrews 12:2).

Jesus saw through his suffering and death to the other side. He saw through the cross to the resurrection. He saw through it all the way to the moment when he would sit down at the throne of God, satisfied with the work he had done to reconcile us to God. What was on the other side of suffering for Jesus? Joy! As Paul was conformed to Jesus' death, we sense his growing confidence in what lay ahead for him on the other side of his death as well, a growing confidence that left him with joy, peace, and hope despite tumultuous circumstances around him. He says in 2 Corinthians 7:4, "I am overflowing with joy in all our afflictions."

Paul spoke of joy in ongoing affliction. Instead, I just wanted my affliction to end. I couldn't fathom how joy could infiltrate my pain. Joy and the affliction hitting my family seemed mutually exclusive. How do we, like Paul, get to that joy in the midst of suffering that refuses to let up? Is such joy a trait only attainable by super-spiritual apostles? How do we move from flailing in Jesus' arms to embracing him with peace and joy as he embraces us?

How do we take up our cross of suffering and follow Jesus anyway?

FELLOWSHIP

Paul used an interesting phrase in his letter to the Philippians when he talked about taking hold of Christ as Christ had taken hold of him. In Philippians 3:10 the phrase *the fellowship of his sufferings* gives us insight into what meditating on Christ offers us in our struggles, something the prophet Isaiah tells us keeps us "in perfect peace" (Isaiah 26:3). The word *fellowship* is key to navigating the alienation we may feel as sufferers and understanding what is provided when we take hold of Christ as he is holding us.

The Greek word Paul uses for this fellowship in suffering is *koinōnia*. It's the same word used for the sweet time early Christians experienced after Pentecost, eating and praying together, and listening to the apostles' teachings (Acts 2:42). The image presented in Acts 2 is the exact opposite of loneliness and alienation. *Koinōnia* can mean communion, intimacy, or intercourse (in the nonsexual sense).[3] While we now use intercourse to refer to sex between two persons, it originally meant sharing ideas or feelings between two persons or groups. In Philippians 1:5 it is translated *partnership*. All of these words give us insight into the understanding that comes from fellowship with Christ in our suffering. He understands and empathizes with us, but as we realize this truth, we grow in our understanding of him as well.

Unlike teaching, fellowship involves a give and take between two persons on equal footing. It is a partnership. A teacher at a college gives information and interacts with a student primarily to see if they have understood the information the teacher gave. The teacher has knowledge superior to the student's. But fellows in an academic setting partner in an activity in a way a teacher and student do not. They are partners working mutually toward the same end goal, helping one another along the way. That contrast helps us see the meaningful things that suffering affords us with Jesus, and what Jesus affords us when suffering. Jesus certainly is our Teacher. But in our suffering, we also find him our partner.

At first, it may sound blasphemous to think of partnering with God the Son in our suffering in the kind of mutual way the Greek word for fellowship suggests. Yet, in keeping with the paradox of the God-man, we find other places in Scripture that use similar common language of God the Son. Notably, in John 15:15, Jesus tells his disciples that he no longer calls them servants, but "I have called you friends, because I have made known to you everything I have heard from my Father." Jesus emptied himself of his rights as God, humbling himself to walk among us in the form of a servant. Jesus didn't come to be served but to serve and give his life a ransom for many (Matthew 20:28). He calls us to serve as he served, fellow servants with God the Son. Jesus condescended to our level in an amazing way. Our God became our friend.

It was this very condescension that Paul wanted to know better, this intimacy with Jesus that suffering allowed him to see and experience. Outside the room of happy, shiny people, Paul found Jesus. Suffering opened the door to Jesus' tent if you will. And Paul was eager to enter it and experience Jesus in the deeper way that suffering allowed. For Jesus' understanding of suffering leads to him equipping us to endure ours, nourishing us like a mother nourishes her child.

PRACTICALLY SPEAKING

In discussing the fellowship of suffering we have with Christ, I have used the metaphorical pictures of turning in Jesus' arms to embrace him as he embraces us, and entering Jesus' tent of refuge where we find understanding, nourishment, and camaraderie. But practically speaking, using real life rather than metaphorical terms, what does it look like to fellowship with Jesus this way? What does it look like for Jesus himself to meet us in our alienation and offer us *koinōnia* with himself?

For me, the first step in actively laying hold of what Jesus has already done for me is to make Paul's prayer at the end of Ephesians 1 mine as well. "I pray that the eyes of your heart may be enlightened so that you may know what is the hope of his calling, what is the wealth of his glorious inheritance in the saints, and what is the immeasurable greatness of his power toward us who believe, according to the mighty working of his strength" (vv. 18-19).

At my worst points of personal pain, my groaning prayer of Ephesians 1:18-19 doesn't sound very eloquent, but the Spirit makes up the difference. Paul prayed that the eyes of the Ephesian believers' hearts would be enlightened. There was truth already at work for those believers, and Paul prayed that their eyes would be opened to understand it. He wanted the light to come on in their hearts and minds so they could see what was already true about them in Christ. I too need my eyes opened to what God is doing that is obscured by the pain of my suffering. I need his help to know him.

When I feel depleted, flattened by suffering, I need God's supernatural help to believe that there is someone holding me up, helping me to function, and restoring my resources with his eternal wealth. I often groan, "Lord, I'm not going to make it." Paul goes on to say in Ephesians 1 that the same power that raised Christ from the grave is the power inside of us, the Holy Spirit. The Holy Spirit will make sure you *do* make it, even when your own resources are so depleted it is impossible for you to make it on your own. Do you feel flattened? Do you feel dead? If so, I encourage you to pray that God would open your eyes to the Holy Spirit's work in you. If you are in Christ, the same agent of resurrection that brought Christ back to life is working in you to set you back on your feet, spiritually, emotionally, and often even physically.

This prayer is key to turning in to Jesus' hold on us. At intense moments of suffering, when things have fallen apart, we need supernatural help to open our eyes to the hope of Christ's call on our lives. We cannot fix our lives. We cannot resurrect ourselves, physically, emotionally, or spiritually. When I find myself flailing, thinking the outcome depends on me, I am frustrated that I cannot resolve whatever I am struggling with in my own power. I need supernatural help to see the wealth of my inheritance through Christ and the greatness of the power of the Holy Spirit to us who believe. To use the tent metaphor, we are actually already sitting with Christ in his warm tent, with nourishing supplies there to aid us, but we are blindfolded, thinking we're alone, oblivious to all at our disposal through our union with him via the Holy Spirit.

In those moments we need to pray that God would remove our blindfold so we can see and experience the very real understanding and nourishment that God alone can provide us when we so desperately need it.

I have found great practical help by following that prayer from Ephesians with a reading from the Gospels, particularly the book of Luke, which includes many of Jesus' interactions with the poor, the shamed, and the stooped—the pariahs of Jesus' time. Note that at the greatest points of pain, I couldn't read much. You may only be able to process a single verse or even just a key phrase. Yet, as reading flows into reading, the story emerges over time. As I read in Luke of Jesus' interactions with real people brought low by their circumstances, I felt communion, *koinōnia*, no longer left on my own to navigate this wilderness of suffering. As believers did in the Gospels, I sensed that I too could take up my cross of suffering and follow Jesus anyway. His yoke is easy, he says in Matthew 11:28-30, and his burden is light. I can take up my cross and follow Jesus because he took up his for me first. Because I am now in him, he bears mine for me too.

Instead of alienation and loneliness, through prayer and reading of Jesus in the Gospels, I realize that I have a partner with me. I have a companion well experienced with grief. There is one who goes before me and you, whose strong arms shelter and feed us. He weeps with us, for he understands our sorrows. But he also guides us and sustains us along the way.

After my mastectomy, which also involved surgery to move skin and muscle from my abdomen to reconstruct my breast, I spent three nights on a pain pump in the ICU in unexpected agony. I could give myself a dose of heavy narcotics every ten minutes. I remember waking up in pain again and again to hit the button on my pump. The sedation helped me fall back into a heavy sleep. But when I woke again in agony, thinking hours had passed, the clock showed that it was only a few minutes since the last time I had awakened. Often, not enough time had passed to give myself more narcotics from the pump. This happened over and over through the night.

I learned when I first woke up from surgery that I had cancer in my lymph node. But the doctor who could tell me more never seemed to stop by my room in the ICU when I was awake. No one seemed to know how bad the cancer was or what I would need to do next.

I had many friends and family who loved and served me well during that hospital stay. Two in particular stayed with me through the night in the ICU, each unable to sleep themselves because of the policies in the ICU. Others stayed with me during the day. But for some reason, that particular night I was alone, in misery, hitting my pain pump every ten minutes, and unable to speak with anyone who could answer the swirl of questions in my head about my cancer. It was the longest night of my life.

The Spirit, though, was with me, and I remember well the moment he prompted me to look at Jesus. Jesus was there, with me in that tent of physical and mental suffering. The gospel hit me in a new way as I was overcome with pain. Jesus empathized with the pain I was feeling. Jesus experienced that level of pain and worse, not to save his own life *but to save mine*. I wept under the covers in that ICU bed, at first at my own pain. But as I meditated, I wept at my new awareness of Jesus' agony in the Garden. And I wept with relief because I realized I wasn't alone.[4]

The Spirit brought to mind scene after scene of Jesus from Scripture that long night. My searing pain pealed layers off of my understanding of what it meant that Jesus was wounded for our transgressions. I saw a nugget of truth previously obscured from my vision. *I* was wounded for my own peace and healing, to save myself from the cancer invading my body. But Jesus received no benefit from his wounding in my place. The Spirit didn't offer me that truth about the extent of Jesus' suffering to make me feel bad about my tears. He wasn't comparing his suffering to mine. "Buck up, Wendy. I've endured way more for you than you are enduring now." Instead, I felt how much Jesus loves me, how much he loves us—he endured that kind of pain to save us from condemnation.

While before surgery, I was blissfully ignorant of the pain I'd soon be enduring, Jesus knew exactly the level of pain he would be facing. He cried out in the Garden of Gethsemane for that cup to pass him by. But it didn't pass by. He endured it anyway, without narcotics to deaden the pain. And he did it not to his own benefit but to ours. Oh, precious Savior!

Those hours of pain, trapped in a hospital bed as Jesus had been to a cross, resulted in the deepest fellowship I have ever felt with him. Jesus helped me endure that night. He nourished me that night. He reminded me that he endured such agony without pain medicine because he loved me. He sustained me through the pain hour after hour, and that memory has equipped me on many days since.

As I continue walking my road of suffering, I am confronted with new stresses that cause me to flail yet again in Jesus' arms. I forget that he holds me securely. I fear I'm going to fall and be trampled by the heavy circumstances I can't navigate on my own. In these moments I am learning to take my thoughts captive, language Paul uses in 2 Corinthians 10:5, and make myself remember that Jesus has me firmly in his grip. I mentally picture turning in his arms as he holds me so I can finish the race held securely by him.

Suffering exposes the truth that Jesus taught in John 15:5—apart from him we can do nothing. But with him, in our deepest moments of pain and struggle, we can find intimate fellowship that equips us for what we could never do individually on our own. Despite our mental distress, we are secure. We have a partner in this treacherous walk, and his love will not let us go.

> He was pierced because of our rebellion,
> crushed because of our iniquities;
> punishment for our peace was on him,
> and we are healed by his wounds. (Isaiah 53:5)

REFLECT

Have you had a previous season of suffering in which you felt you were flailing or in free fall, unable to find your footing? When you reflect back on that time, do you see evidence that God had a hold on you despite your feelings?

What do you think Paul meant in Philippians 3:10-12 when he said he made every effort to take hold of the goal (of knowing Christ and fellowshipping with him in his suffering) because he been taken hold of by Christ Jesus?

What picture comes to mind when you envision yourself taking hold of the truth about Christ as Christ has hold of you?

If knowing Christ this way is your goal, what are some small actions to that end you can take in the midst of long, hard seasons of suffering (when even one small action item can feel overwhelming)?

FELLOWSHIP OF
THE SUFFERING

In my early thirties I became involved with a vibrant, growing church that was reaching many college students and recent graduates. Our community group was full of young couples who quickly became friends with my husband and me. It was an exciting time in our life and ministry. We worshiped together on Sundays and fellowshipped together again midweek. We often gathered at each other's houses for meals in between. We seemed on similar trajectories, figuring out careers and family together as we grew in our faith and understanding of the Bible.

I got pregnant along with my friends from church, many already with toddlers and a few expecting their second. But then I miscarried and had problems getting pregnant again. This led to a season of deep emotional struggle. I felt lonely at times. But even worse, I felt alienated from the community I had freely participated with before. They continued moving forward on their life trajectory, but I felt like I had tripped to a dead stop. This season didn't last long, but it lasted long enough that I took note.

Loneliness involves general feelings of being alone or isolated. But alienation adds a twist of the knife to our loneliness. It involves separation from a person or opportunity we used to have access to. We do not feel alienated from something we were never a part of. We are alienated when we have lost the fellowship or camaraderie we previously enjoyed.

If we move to a new town, we may experience loneliness because we do not yet know people in that town. But if we leave our home church during a church conflict and no longer feel welcome at the places we once shared with our church family, we experience alienation from those who were formerly our friends. We might still see or hear about those we used to share life with, but that only makes the distance between us emotionally and spiritually all the more painful. For those of us who experienced positive social interactions in our work environment, community in our local church, or camaraderie in some other social group before suffering, long seasons of sorrow make us feel less and less a part of something we formerly participated in with enthusiasm. We feel alienated.

Alienation can come from broken relationships, but it can also be a simple result of our circumstances. Surgery followed by six months of chemotherapy, for instance, literally alienates you as you must remove yourself from the people and places you formerly navigated openly because you risk catching a virus or infection that would derail your progress.

During the season of infertility after my miscarriage, I went to a community group dinner at a friend's house. A couple there was expecting their first child, due the same month as the baby I had miscarried. I froze because the pain threatening me by their celebration would undo me if I didn't. But a friend who knew of my miscarriage recognized what was happening to me and took me aside. I don't remember what she said, but I do remember that I realized I wasn't alone, and that singular truth helped me greatly.

After struggling with feelings of alienation about my infertility for a year or so, I got pregnant with my son, and my feelings of alienation resolved in that community. I didn't forget the struggle of that brief season watching everyone around me seemingly flourishing in life as I floundered in mine. And I didn't forget the camaraderie I found with my friend who had suffered in other ways. It was an early lesson in a truth I would need in the longer struggles that faced me a decade later.

LONELY IN A CROWD

I have felt loneliness when I am actually alone. But, like many others, the most profound loneliness with the twisting knife of alienation has occurred when I was surrounded by others. Kate Snow of the *Today Show* observes, "You're surrounded by people, and yet you're feeling lonely. Which I think people don't expect. They think of loneliness as a hermit in a cave who never comes out."[1]

What makes us lonely in a crowd?

During the time when my marriage was disintegrating and again when I was diagnosed with cancer, I found that numerous people with whom I had previously enjoyed social and spiritual interactions felt more and more distant. We could still be in the same room, but it felt like we couldn't talk about the same things. We still sat on the same pew at church, but we seemed to have much less in common.

Was this withdrawing something others did? Was it something I did? Looking back, I realize I changed most of all. I was often unable to laugh and enjoy freely as I had before in social situations, as dark clouds of grief followed me wherever I went. Suffering changed me. It changed my head space. It changed how I looked at the world. It changed how I looked at the happy family sitting beside me in church. I became battle worn, my naive notions of the good Christian life lying in ruins at my feet. In contrast, those with whom I used to interact often seemed unchanged. This reflects the essence of alienation. Whether others were alienating me, or I was alienating myself, the end result was feeling like a pariah, on the outside looking in, no longer able to partake freely in the things I once enjoyed.

The hard truth I have found during my long seasons of struggle, and that fellow sufferers have also testified to, is that relationships with others who aren't suffering really do change. Some folks who aren't suffering may feel threatened by your intense suffering. They can endure with you for a little while, during the season when you still have hope that your suffering will be short term. But when easy solutions fail and you must settle into the marathon of enduring a very long trial, few who haven't suffered long themselves can endure with you. It threatens their own naive notions of what the good Christian life looks like.

But I too alienated myself from others. My church family loved me well. Nevertheless, Sundays at church were my hardest days as I did my best to not run crying from the sanctuary. When well-meaning friends asked how I was doing, I couldn't open myself to talk to them without the dam of my emotions bursting. My choices were to withdraw from conversation on Sundays or weep until I had no more tears. My body couldn't sustain the grief. So I withdrew.

DIS-ABLED TO COMFORT

There is another reason that we may feel alienated in seasons of suffering. In 2 Corinthians 1:3-5, Scripture gives us some insight.

> Blessed be the God and Father of our Lord Jesus Christ, the
> Father of mercies and the God of all comfort. He comforts
> us in all our affliction, so that we may be able to comfort those
> who are in any kind of affliction, through the comfort we
> ourselves receive from God. For just as the sufferings of Christ
> overflow to us, so also through Christ our comfort overflows.

Why is it that those who have not suffered intensely do not have
enduring encouragement to offer those who have? Because, according to Paul, *suffering itself is the conduit to the very ability to comfort.*
Those who have not yet suffered are disabled when it comes to
comforting us in ours. They have not yet learned the ability to
comfort, and that scriptural truth gives us the freedom to not think
badly of those who are unable to endure alongside us with compassion and encouragement we need for the long haul.

More importantly, that truth also reveals to us where to look in
the body of Christ for camaraderie and comfort, for companionship, when we are crushed by the weight of suffering on us. And
hear my exhortation that you do indeed need to proactively look
for such comfort and open yourself to receive it. Paul teaches that
for sufferers there is real comfort from real people in the body of
Christ, comfort that flows directly from Christ himself. We may feel
alienation from some people, but we will not be truly alienated
from all. Where should we look for this comfort from real people?

FELLOW SUFFERERS

In each round of pain I have experienced, I have noticed that
comfort from others doesn't require a one-to-one correlation of
trials. Though I have found some encouragement from divorce-
care ministries or other breast cancer survivors, I have found more

comfort simply from other sufferers. It isn't the fact that they experienced the same kind of trial I experienced but the mere experience of suffering has equipped them with the ability to comfort and encourage me.

During a season of feeling particularly isolated, I remember talking with an elder's wife who shared her story of the fire that burned down her home a few years before. Her family was left with their lives and the clothes on their backs. They lost everything else—pictures, heirlooms, and a lifetime of memories. Though I had never lost a home to fire and this elder's wife had never had breast cancer or been divorced, I found camaraderie with her. She had experienced a loss she could never fully recover. And she could empathize with the ways I had experienced the same.

If you examine 2 Corinthians 1:4 closely, the phrasing gives us insight into the phenomenon I experienced with my church friend and helpful parameters for surviving the alienation that often accompanies suffering. Paul says that God comforts us in *all* of our afflictions, and in return we are equipped to comfort others who are in *any* kind of affliction through the comfort we ourselves received from God. Both "all" and "any" are the same Greek word, *pas*, a word that indicates all sorts of things. In this case, God comforts us in our afflictions, and we then are able to comfort others *in all sorts of* their afflictions. The unifying factor is the universal nature of suffering in general rather than the specific type of suffering itself.

A faithful believer who has endured the loss of her material possessions in a fire has something to offer me as I rebuild my life after divorce and recover from multiple cancer surgeries. No matter the type of suffering, those who have been comforted by God are equipped to comfort others.

Remember the word we examined in chapter two in the discussion of our fellowship with Jesus in his suffering? The Greek word Paul used for this fellowship, this companionship, is *koinōnia*, the same word used for the sweet time early Christians experienced after Pentecost, eating together, praying together, and listening to the apostles teaching of Christ (Acts 2:42).

Second Corinthians 1:3-5 gives us another word with insight to the *koinōnia* available in suffering. The English word is *comfort*, the Greek word *parakaleō*.[2] If you know any biblical Greek, you may recognize that word as close to the one Jesus uses for the Holy Spirit in John 14, *paraklētos*, usually translated "comforter," "counselor," or "helper." Both words have the root *para*, which means to come alongside. But *kaleō* in *parakaleō* indicates a calling or invitation. It's an invitation to come alongside, a welcome to someone to walk together. This simple welcome is the beginning of biblical companionship.

As I found deeper fellowship with Christ as trial piled upon trial in my life, I also found deeper fellowship with those in his body, the church, made up of all who have individually believed in Jesus' name. They were walking their path. I was stumbling along mine. Comfort came through the invitation to walk together.

At first, I was surprised at the way this fellowship and comfort came from brothers and sisters in Christ who had suffered in ways quite different from my own. But 2 Corinthians 1 helped me understand how, the more I personally suffered, I was able to enter others' suffering as they have entered mine even if our circumstances were very different.

Enter is an interesting word for this phenomenon, one that reflects the nuances of *parakaleō*. My friends and I have gone through a doorway that brings us into each others' suffering. We don't sit outside peering in through a window. The biblical model isn't Christians as spectators watching others who suffer exhibited on a stage. We aren't on a stage but invited into a room together, sharing the experience in a way that others who have not suffered cannot. There is a fellowship, companionship, and camaraderie in this room of suffering, though the specifics of our individual experiences differ quite a bit.

When issues were exposed in my home and the specter of separation and divorced loomed over my head, I found particular comfort from two memoirs written by Christian authors of deep faith who experienced very different paths of suffering, *The God of All Comfort* by Dee Brestin and *Washed and Waiting* by Wesley Hill. I felt invited by both authors into their tent of suffering to receive comfort from them as they had received from Christ. Dee's husband was diagnosed with aggressive cancer, dying in his fifties and leaving her in deep grief in the aftermath of his death. Wesley, in contrast, wrestled with his ongoing attraction to the same sex as he submitted to God's commandments regarding sex outside of Christian marriage between a man and a woman.

Despite their very different struggles from each other and from mine, I found great camaraderie and comfort as I read the words they put to their wrestling and struggle. I cried with Dee, but I also rejoiced with her at God's provision through the Scriptures for her emotional well-being. I felt with Wesley the weight of his burdens, and his endurance in hope against temptation to deny the faith steadied me to persevere in my own, particularly when obeying God's commands was costly to me. Both Dee and Wesley came to understand the character of God and his purposes for their lives when their trials and temptations derailed where they once thought they were heading in life, and both came alongside me in aid as I had to do the same.

Dee shared a story of encouragement to persevere in faith from another friend experiencing yet another completely different struggle, a birth defect in her baby son.

"The real battle for Susan was not with spina bifida, but a battle with Satan for a life that would glorify God. Did God truly love her? Was he in control? Or had Jeff's disability happened because the world was spinning out of control under an apathetic or impotent God?"[3] Susan encouraged Dee, "I could see that Satan had to ask for permission to inflict Job, so I knew God was sovereign. I also knew that there was going to be a purpose in Jeff's life and that with God's strength, somehow, we would make it. I desperately needed to know this was not some tragic mistake, but that God had a purpose."[4]

God, through his words to Job, comforted Susan in the diagnosis of her son's spina bifida. Susan in turn shared this comfort with Dee in the death of her husband. And through her book, Dee shared it with me, struggling with yet another set of circumstances distinct from theirs.

"He comforts us in all our affliction, so that we may be able to comfort those who are in any kind of affliction, through the comfort we ourselves receive from God" (2 Corinthians 1:4). I have been comforted by those who have experienced suffering similar to my own, but I have also experienced uncanny fellowship with folks with very different stories. I have been comforted by those still living, but I have also found great support and camaraderie with those who have gone generations before I was born. Suffering itself is the catalyst for this fellowship in the body of Christ, not the specifics of our own individual experience or the time we experienced it.

DEEPER BONDS

When I got the news that my breast cancer had escaped my breast and was found in a lymph node, it knocked me from the peak I thought I had climbed after my initial breast cancer diagnosis. Though I had missed one year of mammograms prior to finding out I had breast cancer, I had been screened frequently before that. Surely this cancer must be early stage. But finding it in a lymph node as well as the breast seemed to change the path forward dramatically.

My brother-in-law, a pastor who has sat with his share of folks in the midst of a crisis, gave me wise advice. He encouraged me to proactively assemble a small team of friends I could be brutally honest with about my burdens. It would exhaust me emotionally to share intimate details of my struggles with too many people. But I wouldn't survive without sharing my burdens at all.

I gathered a group of friends I trusted with my bruised faith and raw emotions. And they have endured with me well. As I look at the ones that have comforted me, I notice a trend. They have suffered in ways distinct from my own. One friend is confined to a wheelchair while facing his own cancer diagnosis. Another was abandoned by her husband while pregnant with their third child. One lost her father to an aggressive form of cancer in the prime of his life, another to a drowning that no one can explain. Several have endured a deeply wounding church conflict that twisted the knife of alienation deep into their and their families' lives. I don't think any of them have been diagnosed with breast cancer while parenting their children alone. But that reflects how this comfort from God works.

In Philippians 3, which we examined in chapter one, Paul talked of the fellowship of suffering in terms of Jesus. We enter his suffering—the man of sorrows, well acquainted with grief—he enters into ours. But Paul also talks of the church as Jesus' body in several of his letters. When I enter another believer's suffering or they enter mine, we are entering into Christ's as well. The fellowship of suffering involves both the Head and the rest of Jesus' body.

> Just as the body is one and has many parts, and all the parts of that body, though many, are one body—so also is Christ. For we were all baptized by one Spirit into one body—whether Jews or Greeks, whether slaves or free—and we were all given one Spirit to drink. Indeed, the body is not one part but many. . . .
>
> So if one member suffers, all the members suffer with it. (1 Corinthians 12:12-14, 26)

What do we gain from fellow believers who have suffered before us—matured and comforted by God—and who then comfort us in our suffering? I can tell you what I have gained from my brothers and sisters in Christ who have comforted me and what you might gain if you gather your own.

- Folks who sit with me and listen rather than offering trite answers or simplistic Christian sayings.

- Friends who pray with me asking God for direction rather than offering advice of their own.

- Friends who can give wisdom on how to be rather than what to do. (Sufferers understand being in a situation where you can't control the outcome; nonsufferers might feel threatened by that idea and have a hard time with anything except advice on how to get out of your suffering.)

- Folks who understand this world is not our home. We are pilgrims on a journey through a dry and weary land, but there is great joy waiting for us eternally in heaven. Suffering exposes the prosperity gospel for the heresy it is.

TALKING ME OFF THE LEDGE

I hesitate to use the phrase *talking me off the ledge* out of concern for those with suicidal loved ones or suicidal thoughts themselves. But it is an accurate metaphor for the emotional and spiritual role these godly companions have played in my life over the last years. I have never stood physically on a ledge, ready to end my life. But in my journey, I have felt many times that I was emotionally and spiritually on a ledge—that if I could have figured out a way to quit the life of faith, I would have. But the words of the disciples in John 6 have been true for me: "Lord, to whom will we go? You have the words of eternal life" (John 6:68).

I haven't left the faith, because God has not let me. I haven't quit, because God won't accept my resignation. I have been kept in the faith by the God who promises he will not lose any of his own. In those moments of despair, friends and family have been God's hands and feet, the body to Jesus' head, who have held me and talked to me until I walked back into the safety of the room, feeling like I could face the overwhelming struggle around me.

I reached this point emotionally again and again in the months leading up to my divorce and subsequent move back to my family on the East Coast and again and again in the weeks after the move back. The enormity of what my boys and I had lost in leaving our life in Seattle, the only city where my children had ever lived, overwhelmed me. I struggled with panic attacks in the weeks leading up to the move and the weeks after. My sisters and two other friends in particular called daily. They listened to me talk through my anxieties, shared with me a verse of Scripture, and prayed with me. Again and again and again. They sat with me in my emotional turmoil, but their faith was strong enough not to feel threatened by my fear and unbelief at the moment.

I remember sitting on the porch of my parents' cabin the week after I moved back to the East Coast, fighting off a panic attack because of the enormity of what I had done. I called my sister, who lived next door, with some panic phrase. "I don't think I'm going to make it." She walked over and sat on the porch with me, speaking truth to me. I can't remember what she said exactly or how long she had to say it, but after some time of reminding me of the truth of God's sovereign care for me and my family, the panic began to lose its grip on my heart again. I could take a deep breath. God was with me. I wasn't an orphan left to figure it all out on my own.

Each of these friends and family members had gone through their own crisis of belief in the midst of suffering, and so they truly empathized with me. They listened and talked me through my panic and anxiety without shame or condemnation that I was in that place (or in that place yet again after talking to them about the exact same struggle a few days before). They understood the point of the angry psalms, God's gift of grace to us who struggle through pain that does not reconcile easily. Most of all, they believed and hoped for me until I could do it again for myself. They prayed for me in hope and confidence in God, and through their prayers God ministered his grace to me.

Like the paralytic man lowered by his friends through the roof to meet Jesus (Mark 2), these friends pointed me to Christ when I felt too weak to seek him on my own. But I had to open myself up to them when I felt ashamed that I couldn't overcome the panic on my own. I had to humble myself before them. God intends such friends to help us in our struggle. They bear our burdens with us when we feel overwhelmed carrying them alone. And they do it as Christ's hands and feet.

We all need friends who will talk us off the emotional ledge, who aren't threatened or horrified by the depths of our deep emotions when we are in crisis. We all need people who will calmly respond to us and help us fact check when we are overcome with emotion. We both need these people in our lives and need to be these people to our friends. "Two are better than one because they have a good reward for their efforts. For if either falls, his companion can lift him up; but pity the one who falls without another to lift him up" (Ecclesiastes 4:9-10).

ADJUSTING TO THE WEIGHT

There comes a moment in long marathons of suffering when you move from efforts to jettison the weight from your shoulders to adjusting the weight so you can carry it for the long haul. Not all trials last all of life. I have been healed from severe foot pain that kept me from being active for several years. But I have not been healed from type 1 diabetes, and I have had to learn how to manage it, knowing that I am likely to wear an insulin pump for the rest of my life.

You can wait in hope for the return to faith of a rebellious child. The wait is agonizing when you don't know when or if they will return to the faith, yet many rebels testify to returning to Christ and reconciling with parents in adulthood. In contrast, a child who dies from cancer is a permanent loss, a weight that cannot be jettisoned from the story of your life. Both weights are impossible to bear if you don't believe in the joy set before you, the destination in eternity that will not disappoint. Sufferers, especially those permanently scarred by circumstances that cannot be undone in this life, get this important truth in a way nonsufferers don't. And their persevering faith becomes a comfort to their brothers and sisters who also suffer. "Behold, I lay in Zion a stone of stumbling and a rock of offense, And he who believes in him will not be disappointed" (Romans 9:33 NASB).

Though Wesley Hill's struggle was in a totally different area of life, the last chapter in *Washed and Waiting,* on his vision for enduring temptation, ministered deeply to me. Similarly, when my friend admonishes me from his wheelchair to not quit; when my suffering sister in Christ reminds me that there is nowhere else to go, for Jesus alone has the words of life; when the woman dying of cancer writes of mundane faithfulness to the bitter end; the companionship in this suffering empowers me to persevere, to count the loss not worthy to be compared to the glory of knowing Christ (Philippians 3:8).

I worship each Sunday in a multicultural church with brothers and sisters in Christ who have endured social stigma and degradation in an area of our nation deeply wounded by racial prejudice and injustice. I missed many weeks of worship after my surgeries, but as I recovered and I dragged myself back to services, I was struck by our corporate worship time.

Despite generations of overt prejudice in our part of the South, our little community of believers joyfully worships God. And I needed that joy. My personal physical exhaustion was mixed with emotional exhaustion after multiple hard years, and I was weary in every sense of that word. The brothers and sisters of our church praise God with joy hard won not from a few years but from generations of hardship. Their parents had worshiped with such joy despite segregation that endured in our area long past the laws that should have ended it. Their grandparents worshiped with similar joy despite experiencing the Jim Crow South firsthand. The joyful perseverance of sisters and brothers in my multicultural church has spoken volumes to me, and I leave our time of worship together comforted with the comfort they have learned through their own struggles and afflictions over generations.

If you are suffering, your first reaction, especially if you are early on in your sorrow, may be to find others whose suffering was reconciled. The estranged couple who worked it out. The cancer patient who recovered. The parents of a rebellious child who saw the child return in faith. But as your suffering continues, you will find a deep treasure in those who have endured without earthly resolution to their pain. Their perseverance will bless you; they know this world is not our home and look to the treasure that lies ahead.

We need such companions. We need others in the body of Christ who have learned joy in the midst of long affliction. Enter into this fellowship with Jesus and with his body. Do not be afraid of it, for this fellowship with persevering brothers and sisters is life-giving. We are not left to walk our road of suffering alone. With fellow sufferers of faith, we will find comfort and nourishment to persevere with hope in our own.

REFLECT

Do you have friends who have suffered in ways similar to or different from your own suffering who have come alongside you? How have they been helpful to you?

Have you been able to be that kind of friend to someone else in their journey of suffering? How are you *able* to comfort others in ways you weren't before your journey of suffering?

Have you found camaraderie with the author of a book who suffered differently from you? What about their description of their own journey has been helpful to you?

If you don't have a group of friends walking with you, do you know acquaintances who profess a sincere faith in Christ who have suffered? Consider asking them if you can share your burdens or prayer requests with them regularly.

PLEADING FOR RESCUE

Fellowship with King David

"I'm praying through Psalm 69 for you."

I received this text from a friend with whom I shared my deepest emotional burdens and spiritual fatigue, one of the group I assembled in light of my brother-in-law's advice. I was driving home after sitting with my dad—a dear support to me as I worked to find my way forward as a single mom—who now lay in the ICU on a ventilator at a teaching hospital two cities away. Between my second and third cancer surgery, he nearly died after doctors punctured his lung and nicked a vein during a heart procedure. He already had congestive heart failure, and his heart struggled to recover. On top of that, I was scheduled to begin five weeks of daily radiation following my mastectomy the Monday after he landed in the intensive care unit. The multiple layers of weight—my dad on a ventilator, cancer in my lymph node, stress from my divorce—along with all the sorrows, fears, and responsibilities that came with each, pressed me down. Yet, despite the weights, I had no choice but to move forward. The medical pressures of life for either my dad or myself would not wait on me to feel emotionally stable to face them.

The sister in Christ who sent me this text was one who was *able* to comfort me, a living believer equipped by her own suffering to minister to me as the hands and feet of Jesus. She then pointed me to the next level of companionship I desperately needed in my trials, companionship in the Scriptures. Scripture feels daunting when we are in dark places of suffering, but it claims to have supernatural power (Hebrews 4:12). When we are in our darkest places of suffering, we desperately need its supernatural power.

A PLEA FOR RESCUE

When my friend sent me that text, I was confused about what psalm she was referencing. Though I had read through the Bible many times, Psalm 69 was not on my radar. Psalms 1, 23, 51, 73, 119, and 150 all were. Many others were also well marked in my Bible. But not Psalm 69. In fact, when I turned to it in my Bible, it only had the briefest of marks on it. If it had drawn my attention before, it didn't make a lasting impression at the time. It is interesting how a change in life circumstances can be a conduit to seeing truth from Scripture you never noticed before. Psalm 69 has now become a precious resource to me, a balm to my soul with language to bring directly to God in prayer. When I didn't know how to verbalize my prayers to God under the weight of the pressures of this season in my life, God reminded me through this psalm that he hadn't left me as an orphan to figure it out on my own. He gave me a companion in King David to give language to my anguish.

In the Christian Standard Bible, Psalm 69 is titled "A Plea for Rescue." In contrast, I am familiar with Scripture on persevering in suffering. I need verses about enduring the marathon of life, about the fruit that grows as we persevere in the faith. But at particularly intense points, when it is hard to catch our breath and we feel our own hearts lurch, we need rescue. God preserved such a plea, not for perseverance but for actual rescue, for us in his eternal Word. He guarded it throughout the ages so that you and I in the twenty-first century would have the language to cry out to God for not just endurance but actual rescue when we struggle to form a coherent thought. King David gives us aid through this prayer, becoming the hands and feet of God to us, as he models how to righteously cry out to God in the midst of deep emotional agony.

David prayed,

> Save me, God,
> for the water has risen to my neck.
> I have sunk in deep mud, and there is no footing;
> I have come into deep water,
> and a flood sweeps over me.
> I am weary from my crying;
> my throat is parched.
> My eyes fail, looking for my God.
> Those who hate me without cause
> are more numerous than the hairs of my head;
> my deceitful enemies, who would destroy me,
> are powerful.
> Though I did not steal, I must repay. (Psalm 69:1-4)

One of the gifts God gives us through David in Psalm 69 is the way he articulates his dark emotions. We are not sure which low point prompted David to write this psalm, but he had many dark times in his life. He had dark nights of the soul because of God's anointing of him to be the future king. He hid in a cave fearing for his life as King Saul sought to kill him. But David experienced dark nights of the soul as a consequence of his own sin as well. He lost a child after he sinned deeply against Bathsheba and Uriah. He later failed to discipline his other children and suffered greatly at the hands of his son Absalom as a result of the chaos that ensued.

King David sat in the tent of suffering as we do now. In Psalm 69, he had sunk deep in his circumstances and emotions, and he could not find a foothold. He was floundering, feeling that he was about to drown. He was running out of tears, not because the sorrow had eased but *because his body could not physically sustain his sorrow anymore.*

I find camaraderie with David in this feeling. I've experienced such emotional exhaustion more often than I would like. That feeling doesn't usually sweep over me at the exact moment I hear some grievous news but descends in the hours and days after I process what exactly this new round of relational or medical turmoil means for me. I remember walking the dirt loop of the driveway around my house on our family farm after the call came that I had breast cancer. Walking the farm has been an activity I've turned to again and again as I process new information or wrestle with old issues that won't go away. A nurse called me Friday afternoon, but I couldn't meet with the doctor until Tuesday. I walked and walked and walked that loop in the days in between, whispering to myself, "I'm not going to make it."

I was a single parent trying to help my own aging parents with their health problems, and they in turn were trying to help me. I didn't have enough information to know how serious my cancer was, but even in the best-case scenario, it meant physical burdens for months to come. My emotions were flatlining. How could I keep my head above the waters? How could I help my loved ones from my own hospital bed? How could I pay my bills if I couldn't work? Why was God allowing this to happen to me? I was the smoldering wick about to flicker out (Matthew 12:20).

As a woman raised from youth in the church, I find myself at times feeling guilt in such moments. *Of course I'm going to make it. I've got God on my side. Greater is he that is in me than he that is in the world. I'm an overcomer.* And so forth. I know all of the pick-me-up passages from Scripture quite well.

But in the moments of our deepest sorrows and fears, spiritual pep talks cannot cut through the heavy veil of fear and grief. We need more than a pep talk. We need spiritual nourishment. Like a starving wanderer pulled from the desert right before they die, we may need to be spoon-fed the most basic sustenance. Through Psalm 69, King David spoon-fed me a prayer when I was at a very low point, when I couldn't come up with words for myself. And it started, befitting the theme of this book, by offering me simple fellowship with God's anointed king of Israel who, in turn, pointed me toward God himself.

If you feel you are about to drown in your suffering, you too are not alone. If your tears have dried up simply because your body can no longer sustain physical outpourings of sorrow, you have comrades in the faith. David, the greatest earthly king of God's children, a man after God's own heart, struggled as we do. He felt deep, dark emotions, and God didn't rebuke him for it. Instead, God preserved his cry eternally for us as a model of prayer, as a plea for rescue.

THE OTHER PROSPERITY GOSPEL

David ends verse 4 with a poignant statement that has encapsulated the grief and consternation I have felt at multiple points in my journey, "Though I did not steal, I must repay." This is helpful language for earnest believers recovering from the prosperity gospel of conservative evangelicals.

Though many Christians mock the health, wealth, and prosperity gospel and the name-it-and-claim-it televangelists who make their millions off it, we still often attach an expectation of good earthly outcomes to wise instructions in the Bible. I was taught that I would save myself a heap of trouble if I were careful to make good decisions, particularly regarding marriage, family, and work. As an earnest young Christian, I took that advice seriously, but the heap of trouble found me regardless.

I thank God for youth groups and Bible colleges that taught me scriptural wisdom. But we set ourselves up for a rude awakening when we confuse such biblical *wisdom* with Bible *promises*. There is wisdom in obedience to God's commands, but it is not a guarantee that no ill will befall us in life. In Psalm 69, David reminds us that being a man after God's own heart didn't result in a pain-free life. In the particular circumstances of Psalm 69, David was in part paying in suffering what he did not owe from disobedience.

In the next section of this psalm, David acknowledged his own foolishness. He was not completely innocent in the confluence of circumstances that brought him so low. But he also endured insults because of his righteous love for God. At multiple points in his life he endured oppression and humiliation as a result of God's call on his life to be king of Israel. In verse 4 David articulated a key burden I have struggled with at each turn in my own trials—the seeming unfairness of it all. Why am I paying someone else's debt? And the other angle to that question—why aren't I enjoying the profit from my own righteous investments? I squash such thoughts down when they arise in my mind. They feel very unspiritual. But David's cry to God gives me permission to name this struggle and face it head-on. Suffering feels keenly unfair when it seems to leave us paying the consequences of a sin someone else committed.

PLEADING FOR FAVOR

Though the specific causes and circumstances of David's suffering are unknown to us and likely different from ours, in verses 13-18 he uses language that reflects the struggle I have faced in my suffering again and again.

> But as for me, LORD,
> my prayer to you is for a time of favor.
> In your abundant, faithful love, God,
> answer me with your sure salvation.
> Rescue me from the miry mud; don't let me sink.
> Let me be rescued from those who hate me
> and from the deep water.
> Don't let the floodwaters sweep over me
> or the deep swallow me up;
> don't let the Pit close its mouth over me.
> Answer me, LORD,
> for your faithful love is good.
> In keeping with your abundant compassion,
> turn to me.
> Don't hide your face from your servant,
> for I am in distress.
> Answer me quickly!
> Come near to me and redeem me;
> ransom me because of my enemies. (Psalm 69:13-18)

When my friend first drew my attention to this psalm and I began meditating on it in earnest, I was drawn again and again to

David's prayer for "a time of favor." It struck a nerve for me. Despite pastoral counsel and the encouragement of friends, I have often struggled with the feeling that I am out of favor with God. Is this the reason that I sit under the weight of seemingly unfair trials? Has God removed his favor from me? Did I ever have it to begin with? Those questions reflect the core emotional burden I have felt, second-guessing every decision I've made, self-chastising for the most minor perceived shortcomings. I've certainly made mistakes along my journey, but did I bring all of this on myself?

Though others looking at my life from the outside affirm my faithfulness to God, and I am in good standing with my church elders, I have struggled with tremendous self-doubt, particularly related to my divorce. Suffering does this to earnest believers. What did I do wrong to get myself in this situation? How did I get out of God's favor, and more importantly, how do I get back into it?

I long to find my way back into God's good graces. Thankfully, God left us the story of Job to meet us in exactly this mental burden, and we will examine that righteous man's suffering more in later chapters. But, for now, let's consider the language David used in Psalm 69 and how the Scriptures meet us with this deep emotional burden, our longing for respite, even blessing, a time of favor with God.

The Hebrew word for "favor" is *ratson*, derived from *ratsah*, which means to be pleased with or to have satisfied a debt.[1] In other places in Scripture, the same phrase for "time of favor" is translated "an acceptable time." It is a phrase used in Messianic prophecies, such as Isaiah 49.

This is what the LORD says:
    I will answer you in a time of favor,
    and I will help you in the day of salvation. . . .

[S]aying to the prisoners: Come out,

and to those who are in darkness: Show yourselves.

They will feed along the pathways,

and their pastures will be on all the barren heights.

They will not hunger or thirst,

the scorching heat or sun will not strike them;

for their compassionate one will guide them,

and lead them to springs. (Isaiah 49:8-9)

In the New Testament, the apostle Paul clears this up for us when he quotes this language from Isaiah 49 in his letter to the church at Corinth: "See, now is the acceptable time [of favor]; now is the day of salvation!" (2 Corinthians 6:2).

Paul says the time of favor is upon us as he disciples the church at Corinth in the grace of God through Christ. What does this word *ratson* or *favor* indicate? What was David longing for that we now have in Christ? This Bible word indicates God's acceptance of us, delight in us, and goodwill toward us.[2]

The New Testament teaches that we are now in a time of God's favor and acceptance. Why does God delight in us? How did God see fit to extend to us this divine good will? He extended it through Christ! The time of favor and good will is upon all who believe in Christ, the apostle Paul declares. Jesus came at the acceptable time, and he ushered in a time of favor for all who believe in his resurrection and confess him as Lord (Romans 10:9-10).

How does this favor break into the long season of suffering you find yourself in? How does it break into mine? It starts by removing any condemnation we may feel. "Therefore, there is now no condemnation for those in Christ Jesus" (Romans 8:1).

As I said, I've struggled with shame and self-condemnation again and again throughout my trials. Surely there must have been something more I could have done to avoid my divorce or my cancer diagnosis. What signs did I miss? What balls did I drop? But though there can be natural consequences to our bad choices, we also know Christ has fully satisfied our debt to God. David cried out in agony in Psalm 69:4 as he paid the debt of another's theft, but Jesus turned the score around. He repaid our debt. He fulfilled Psalm 69:4, paying back what we have stolen. The result, as Isaiah 49:8-9 poetically portrays, is the restoration of our desolate places and an invitation to come out of the dark shadows and show ourselves in the light. We are no longer pariahs.

If I missed a sign as my marriage failed, Christ read it for me. If I dropped a ball with my physical health, Christ picked it up.

I rightly confess my sins, for I have not walked any path in my life in perfect obedience. But I also put away self-condemnation, for Christ has paid any condemnation for me and offers me peace in its place.

HOPE THAT ANCHORS

This time of favor we have in Christ also gives us hope that anchors us in the middle of long trials.

> Therefore, since we have been declared righteous by faith, we have peace with God through our Lord Jesus Christ. We have also obtained access through him by faith into this grace in which we stand, and we rejoice in the hope of the glory of God. And not only that, but we also rejoice in our afflictions, because we know that affliction produces endurance, endurance produces proven character, and proven character produces hope. *This hope will not disappoint us,* because God's

love has been poured out in our hearts through the Holy Spirit who was given to us. (Romans 5:1-5, emphasis added)

The prosperity gospel disappoints sufferers. It teaches that God's good will toward me depends on my juggling circumstances correctly. If that's the case, I am sunk. But, in Christ, you and I have something altogether different. We have a hope that will not disappoint us, that will not let us down. There is something about our access to God through Christ and the peace we have with him as a result that will see us through, that will not leave us hanging. That will not disappoint.

The mixture of Messianic prophecy in Psalm 69, such as mentioning the vinegar and gall given to Christ on the cross (v. 21), along with David's cry for a time of favor and rescue, is incredibly helpful. It plops us back in the tent of suffering from chapter two; it takes the blindfold off and points out the rescue we have through this one who sits with us, sustaining us as we wait on all things to be made new. As we fellowship with David in Psalm 69, he helps us see Christ anew.

In verses 13-14, and 18, David cried,

> Answer me with your sure salvation.
> Rescue me from the miry mud; . . .
> Come near to me. . . .
> Redeem me;
> Ransom me.

If you have been a believer for any length of time, you recognize these spiritually loaded words (emphasis is mine).

- I am not ashamed of the gospel, because it is the power of God for *salvation* to everyone who believes. (Romans 1:16)

- He has *rescued* us from the domain of darkness and transferred us into the kingdom of the Son he loves. (Colossians 1:13)

- Now in Christ Jesus, you who were far away have been *brought near* by the blood of Christ. (Ephesians 2:13)

- He gave himself for us to *redeem* us from all lawlessness and to cleanse for himself a people for his own possession. (Titus 2:14)

- For even the Son of Man did not come to be served, but to serve, and to give his life as a *ransom* for many. (Mark 10:45)

Save. Rescue. Redeem. Ransom. We know who redeemed David, and we know who ransoms us. We know who turned toward us, and we know who answered both David and us with sure salvation. Most of all, believers know who paid the debt that we each owed. The one given vinegar for his thirst on the cross (Psalm 69:21) has done all of this for us, and that is the truth that serves as a hydraulic lift under our feet when we are sinking in the mire, a lift that slowly but surely raises us back up.

The problem for those in the midst of long seasons of suffering is that while Scripture says we are rescued and redeemed by Christ, our circumstances don't reinforce that truth right now. My feet still seem to be sinking in the miry mud. I am waiting for rescue from the weights on me, not celebrating that they have already been lifted. I'm thankful for the language of Christ in Hebrews 2 that captures this seeming disconnect: "In subjecting everything to him, he left nothing that is not subject to him. As it is, we do not yet see everything subjected to him" (Hebrews 2:8).

Suffering friend, though you do not yet see everything made right, you are not out of favor with God. Cling to the hope that you are, in Christ, in full favor with God. We live in the tension between what we already know to be true in Christ, that he puts away all of our tears and rights all wrongs, and the reality of life in a fallen world. Though we have not yet seen Jesus' kingship fully realized in our world or even in our own private lives, his promise to us is that we will not ultimately be disappointed by our faith in him. His kingdom will fully come, and he is a very good King.

TAKE HEART

After more messianic language and calling down God's wrath on evildoers, David ends Psalm 69 with the word of encouragement we need. David speaks a good word to us as much as any friend in person might. Though the hydraulic platform of God's sure salvation hasn't yet lifted David out of his miry circumstances, it has lifted him out of his miry head space. He ends this psalm with his head and heart firmly set in the reality of the hope that will not disappoint, even if his circumstances haven't yet caught up. And he turns toward us in this psalm and encourages us to do the same.

> You who seek God, take heart!
> For the LORD listens to the needy
> and does not despise
> his own who are prisoners.
> Let heaven and earth praise him,
> the seas and everything that moves in them,
> for God will save Zion
> and build up the cities of Judah.
> They will live there and possess it.
> The descendants of his servants will inherit it,
> and those who love his name will live in it. (Psalm 69:32-36)

Take heart, friend. The Lord listens to your cries. He doesn't despise you when you are down and out. He sees you and me, and he will save us. Though we suffer for a season, we will inherit an over-flowing surplus of good things.

Fundamentally, Psalm 69 is a prayer that we won't drown. And though my circumstances haven't all resolved the way I had hoped, I can confidently say that I haven't drowned. The things that I thought would destroy me did not actually destroy me. God doesn't always save my bank account or my health. But he does save my soul. You have the same hope in Christ.

Through my friend's text, this living fellow sufferer pointed me to another sufferer who had lived and died thousands of years before me. King David then spoke to me through words eternally preserved by God. When I plea, "Rescue me," King David speaks strong words of encouragement back to me, "Take heart! The Lord hears you, and he doesn't despise you for crying out your need. He will save you. You will live in the good land he is preparing for you. Take heart. You will not be disappointed."

REFLECT

Read through Psalm 69 on your own. What phrases used by David at this low point in his life reflect how you feel in your own?

Have you felt that you were repaying a debt you did not owe? In what ways?

Paul says in 2 Corinthians 6:2 that the time of favor is upon us now that Christ has come. Yet Hebrews 2:8 says that we do not yet see everything fully subjected to Jesus as King. How do these two simultaneous truths equip you to walk your particular road of suffering?

HELP MY UNBELIEF

Fellowship with Asaph

In college, I faced my first deep crisis of belief. I had come to Christ years before and had a strong desire to serve God, which resulted in enrolling at a Christian university. But shortly after arriving, I began to seriously doubt the truth of the Bible.

A chasm opened in front of me, and I could not see a way around it. I felt as if I were about to fall into a pit without a bottom. How could I survive without confidence in the Scriptures? How could I believe the Scriptures if I couldn't prove them true?

Over the next months, God gifted me with the faith I needed to move forward. And I have since come to have great confidence in the Scriptures. But that emotional chasm reopened at my cancer diagnosis. The best way I can describe it is that my cancer diagnosis didn't compute. I had gone through a cancer scare in the same breast a few years before, and we monitored it closely. But multiple years of tests confirmed it was not cancer. In fact, the Lord had seemed to guard my entire family from an unexplained cancer diagnosis. Sisters, aunts, uncles, great aunts, and great uncles had no history of cancer. My mom developed breast cancer in the years before doctors realized its link to high doses of estrogen. But she recovered well, and blood relatives in my extended family had virtually no other cancer diagnoses. Yet here I was. It didn't make sense with what I thought I understood about my God or what I understood about my body. What other confident beliefs would turn out to be false? Beliefs about both God and myself that had felt strong and secure for decades suddenly felt on very shaky ground.

In Psalm 73, God preserved the words of the psalmist Asaph, a musician and worship leader in Israel who was also at the edge of a deep chasm of unbelief. Though long dead, Asaph is another believer who offers us companionship as we suffer today. Like Psalm 69, Asaph gives us language for bringing our raw emotions to God and finding in him both comfort and resources to move forward. I have found community with this psalmist as I have with King David. We don't know Asaph's exact circumstances, but there are hints throughout his words of the kind of unrelenting stress and pressure that long-term sufferers know all too well.

He begins,

> God is indeed good to Israel,
> to the pure in heart.
> But as for me, my feet almost slipped;
> my steps nearly went astray. (Psalm 73:1-2)

What a succinct summary of the struggle earnest believers feel in long periods of suffering and trial. Asaph affirms that God is good to Israel, to those who are pure in heart. He knows the truth about the character of God and holds to good theology. But there is a grave disconnect between verses 1 and 2, between what he says he believes about God and the reality of his feelings on the ground. I identify with Asaph in these feelings, and I am deeply thankful God moved him to write these words. Asaph's knowledge of God, though true, isn't breaking into the issues he is facing in his earthly life. Like David in Psalm 69, his body can no longer sustain the pressures of his journey. While David felt like he was drowning, Asaph felt as if he were on the verge of falling to his spiritual death. Both were at the end of their rope.

Why was Asaph about to slide off the path of faith and righteousness into an unknown pit?

DESPAIR

> For I envied the arrogant;
> I saw the prosperity of the wicked.
> They have an easy time until they die,
> and their bodies are well fed.
> They are not in trouble like others;
> they are not afflicted like most people. (Psalm 73:3-5)

For a worship leader well acquainted with the truths of God, verse 3 is a heavy admission. Asaph sees the prosperity of the wicked and envies them. Like many long-term sufferers before and since, he is experiencing the death of whatever prosperity gospel he believed. Is he watching other faithful Jews around him suffer in the shadow of wicked abundance? Is he experiencing this affliction personally? Whichever way, the worst of humanity seems to have a much better life than he. They are well fed, enjoying an easy time, while Asaph or those he loves are troubled and afflicted. This reality has brought him very low. His feet and his faith are slipping. I identify with his discouragement.

> Therefore, pride is their necklace,
>
> and violence covers them like a garment.
>
> Their eyes bulge out from fatness;
>
> the imaginations of their hearts run wild.
>
> They mock, and they speak maliciously;
>
> they arrogantly threaten oppression. (Psalm 73:6-8)

The picture painted in these verses reveals Asaph's proximity to those prospering by oppressing the righteous. Maybe he labors in their courts or works in their fields. Whatever the circumstance, Asaph is watching this injustice from a painfully close vantage point. He can see their eyes bulging with fatness. They wear their pride like a necklace. It is their decoration, their embellishment. They don't even pretend token humility. They are verbally malicious, threatening oppression out of sheer meanness. And from verse 7, we gather they enjoy their gluttony while Asaph's foot is slipping and his faith is shaking.

> They set their mouths against heaven,
>
> and their tongues strut across the earth.
>
> Therefore his people turn to them
>
> and drink in their overflowing words.
>
> The wicked say, "How can God know?
>
> Does the Most High know everything?" (Psalm 73:9-11)

Asaph's disillusionment is clear. He laments that the wicked "set their mouths against heaven." They do not shake their rebellious fist only at people on earth; they shake their fist at the God of gods in heaven, seemingly without consequence.

To compound Asaph's struggle, as the wicked challenge his theology, others turn toward them. Those who should believe the truth about God with the psalmist are instead drinking in the wicked's blasphemy. "God doesn't know," they say. They mock God as impotent and unaware. Like a stranded swimmer unable to get the attention of the ship that passes by, a believer experiences utter demoralization when they sense God passing by them without awareness or knowledge of their need. "He doesn't even know I'm sick or hurting or scared or starving." Such a false view of God's impotence or unawareness causes deep despair. If you have felt that, Asaph reminds us we do not sit in that tent of despair alone.

> Look at them—the wicked!
> They are always at ease,
> and they increase their wealth.
> Did I purify my heart
> and wash my hands in innocence for nothing?
> For I am afflicted all day long
> and punished every morning.
> If I had decided to say these things aloud,
> I would have betrayed your people. (Psalm 73:12-15)

Asaph pours out his weariness in verses 12 and 13. The wicked are *always* at ease, increasing in wealth. They are rewarded for their sin, it seems to him in his weariness. He cries out in anguish as I have done myself, "Did I purify my heart for nothing?" "Did I follow you from youth, God, only to have my family and life destroyed?" Like Asaph, I have felt punished at times for the bad choices of others, paying back what I did not owe as David felt in Psalm 69. What was the point of obeying God if I was going to have to bear the consequences for someone else's sin regardless?

According to verse 15, Asaph was feeling things internally that he could not verbalize to others because he knew if he said what he was really thinking, it would seem to be a betrayal of everything he was supposed to believe about God. Does that sound familiar?

I have been there multiple times through these long years since I recognized the path of suffering in front of me and my family. I have at times faked it on the outside because I did not want to betray God or those I love by acknowledging how vain, empty, and meaningless my belief in God seemed at certain moments. I thank God for this psalm and the solidarity in the sorrows of suffering I have found with Asaph. He has given me language for deep emotions I didn't know how to articulate, and Psalm 73 has given me permission to bring those emotions to God as Asaph did, preserved in God's Word for us all these years later.

Do you identify with Asaph's despair? Perhaps you stood strong for a while during trying circumstances, but at some point, as the stresses piled up, the weight on you finally seemed to push you off the edge, unable to get a foothold to keep from falling. Maybe, even as you read this now, you feel like you have slipped off the edge, hanging at the end of your rope, unable to find a foothold. If you can't find a foothold, know first that you are not alone. Many others have stood at this chasm, and Asaph offers us a foothold and a hand to get back to firmer ground.

HOPE

There are a few moments in Scripture where the words paint in vivid detail the contrast between our devastating need and God's overwhelming provision, between the end we have come to in ourselves and the unstoppable power of God's hydraulic lift that catches and raises us back up. This moment in Psalm 73 is one that strikes me every time I read it.

When I tried to understand all this,

it seemed hopeless

until I entered God's sanctuary.

Then I understood their destiny. (Psalm 73:16-17)

The psalmist felt completely hopeless as he tried to reconcile all he saw. His hopelessness in verse 16 makes the provision in verse 17 all the more beautiful.

Asaph entered God's sanctuary, and everything made sense—simple but profound words. Asaph entered the temple, but the presence of God was mediated through priests offering sacrifices on behalf of those who came to worship. As New Testament believers with the whole revelation of Jesus Christ, Christ's death on the cross purchased free access to God's throne room for all who believe. Understanding how Jesus gives us access to God is worth a short diversion from Psalm 73 into the New Testament to explore this access to God we now have that changed everything for Asaph.

THE HOLIEST SANCTUARY

In Asaph's time, the temple of God consisted of an outer courtyard where common people were allowed and an inner sanctuary where only priests were allowed. Within this inner sanctuary was the most holy place. It housed the Ark of the Covenant, God's symbolic presence with his people, which held the Ten Commandments God gave to Moses on Mount Sinai. There was a thick curtain between this most holy place (and God's presence with the people) and the area where the priests were allowed. Once a year, the high priest entered this most holy place with severe restrictions. He had to offer a blood sacrifice and undergo ritual cleansing. Even after rigorous preparations, tradition taught that the other priests attached a rope to his ankle so they could pull him out in the event he entered unworthily and God struck him dead.

At the climactic moment of Christ's death on the cross, he cried out, "It is finished!" Matthew 27:51 says that, at that moment, "the curtain of the sanctuary was torn in two from top to bottom." The heavy, thick barrier between the children of God and God's symbolic presence with them was ripped apart. The doorway to God's presence was opened wide. The author of Hebrews is intent that we understand the significance of what Christ accomplished for us at that moment: "Therefore, let us approach the throne of grace with boldness, so that we may receive mercy and find grace to help us in time of need" (Hebrews 4:16).

> Therefore, brothers and sisters, since we have boldness to enter the sanctuary through the blood of Jesus—he has inaugurated for us a new and living way through the curtain (that is, through his flesh)—and since we have a great high priest over the house of God, let us draw near with a true heart in full assurance of faith, with our hearts sprinkled clean from an evil conscience and our bodies washed in pure water. (Hebrews 10:19-22)

In Christ, we can enter God's presence with boldness. We do not enter the presence of our King like Esther did with Xerxes, fearing for her life. We do not need to enter bearing a new sacrifice or our own good works. Instead, we are exhorted to come boldly and confidently to receive *mercy* and *grace* in our *time of need*. We do this privately as we read Scripture on our own and come to God in private prayer, but we do this corporately as well when we gather together to worship God as a church. We find a foothold and a hand up to firmer ground through these moments of bold access to God.

VISION RESTORED

As Hebrews 4:16 teaches will happen, the weary writer of Psalm 73 found great mercy and grace in his time of need by entering the sanctuary of God. At the temple Asaph likely experienced the reading of God's Word and the testimony of God's faithfulness from others of God's children. Maybe he heard the leader repeat from Psalm 136, "His faithful love endures forever," over and over again. Whatever he experienced as he entered the sanctuary of God, much changed for him as a result.

Consider all that changed, not in his circumstances, but in his perspective after he entered the sanctuary of God.

Indeed, you put them in slippery places;
you make them fall into ruin.
How suddenly they become a desolation!
They come to an end, swept away by terrors.
Like one waking from a dream,
Lord, when arising, you will despise their image.
(Psalm 73:18-20)

In one sense, nothing had changed for Asaph. And yet everything had. He had been wearing out-of-focus glasses that were distorting his vision of life. When he entered the presence of God, he got new lenses and his vision was restored. Finally, Asaph understood the destiny of the wicked. He saw their prosperity in an entirely different light. He comprehended the truth of where they were heading, and it would be utter ruin. When God finally roused himself against them, it would be devastating. We too need these new lenses.

In the long, slow painful months leading up to and after my divorce, I couldn't process long passages of Scripture. My mind fluttered to and fro, wondering what I could do differently, feeling guilt for mistakes I had made, and fearfully contemplating the struggles of the future. Counselors and therapists helped me work through my emotions. Elders in my church guided me compassionately. But daily, I benefited from psalms such as Psalm 73. I could sit in the psalms and find companionship and help. Like Asaph, I needed help settling my mind. It may have been a chapter, a verse, or just a phrase, but again and again, the psalms helped me. Throughout the history of the church, believers have found Psalms true help at the worst points of suffering in life. Perhaps, at particularly hard seasons, you can keep a psalter close to your bed, one you can open and read (or have someone read to you) at your lowest points.

Like Asaph in Psalm 73, I know when my perspective on the evil around me has been restored by the presence of God. It is that moment when I stop being jealous of the wicked and start feeling burdened for them. Those experiencing the betrayal of divorce may benefit from this in particular. I have a close friend whose husband left her for a wealthy woman, devastating their family and leaving my friend in financial ruin. For a long time it seemed simply a bitter betrayal. I remember the day she told me for the first time, not in anger or codependence but with heartfelt compassion, how concerned she was for him and the path his choices were taking him. It is only the clear perspective that comes from the presence of God that gives us such clarity on the terror of living apart from him.

In 2 Timothy 2:24-26, Paul gives us an additional perspective on the wicked: "The Lord's servant must not quarrel, but must be gentle to everyone, able to teach, and patient, instructing his opponents with gentleness. Perhaps God will grant them repentance leading them to the knowledge of the truth. Then they may come to their senses and escape the trap of the devil, who has taken them captive to do his will."

Paul reminded Timothy that the wicked on earth were not his ultimate enemy. They were enslaved by the real enemy, Satan. Paul's instructions remind us today to hope for the repentance of those who oppose us and their escape from Satan who has taken them captive to do his will. Only time in the presence of God will give us that perspective on our enemies and move us from vexation over their prosperity to concern for their final destiny. This is one of the great mental helps we get from our access to God and his sanctuary through the veil ripped in two by Christ's sacrifice.

Asaph continues:

> When I became embittered
> and my innermost being was wounded,
> I was stupid and didn't understand;
> I was an unthinking animal toward you. (Psalm 73:21-22)

Not only was Asaph's perspective adjusted so that he saw the wicked clearly, but he also had a clearer understanding of himself. Prior to entering God's sanctuary, he felt quite sorry for himself. But now Asaph recognizes that his lament was mixed with his own bitterness and ignorance. He had been stupid—a striking rebuke to himself. He had been responding more like an unthinking animal than an image bearer of God. Have you had a moment when you came to your senses as Asaph did? I have.

Asaph reminds me that I am not always a righteous sufferer. I sometimes say foolish things about God, and sometimes I sin against others in my frustration at my own circumstances. But there is great beauty and grace in the next verses even as he confesses his ignorance and bitterness.

> Yet I am always with you;
> you hold my right hand.
> You guide me with your counsel,
> and afterward you will take me up in glory.
>   (Psalm 73:23-24)

Though Asaph had been ignorant and bitter with God, he did not wallow in self-condemnation. He had no need to live in shame. He didn't deride himself again and again. Instead, he confessed his sin and unbelief, got up, and walked forward in the truth hand in hand with God.

I have not been a sinless sufferer. I have sometimes lashed out at others in frustration. I have at times lashed out at God. I have been envious of the wicked and embittered by the turn my life has taken. It is humbling to admit my sin, especially when I am already brought low by the weight of circumstances on me. But in Christ, admitting my sin doesn't bring me lower! There is no condemnation for those who are in Christ Jesus (Romans 8:1). Like Asaph, I can face my sin and unbelief head on, confess it, and get up with my small hand tucked firmly into God's much larger one, for Christ has taken the weight of my sin and clothed me instead with his righteousness (2 Corinthians 5:21). His punishment has bought my peace. By his wounds, I have been healed.

In verses 23 and 24, Asaph succinctly reviews the three-pronged attributes of God that are foundational to good theology. God is sovereign, God is wise, and God is compassionate.[1] Asaph knew the truth of God's character in verse 1 of Psalm 73, but here his confidence in this truth is restored. His theology has once again broken into the reality of his life, the disconnect between verses 1 and 2 is fixed. His theology is practical once again.

After entering the sanctuary of God, Asaph, the worship leader, felt the truth of God's love and compassion for him. He felt God holding him by the hand like a child, guiding him with his wise counsel. And after this life he was confident that his sovereign God would take him to glory. Asaph knew he wouldn't be disappointed by his hope in God.

With his refocused perspective, this psalmist had his eye on the eternal. Throughout the Old and New Testaments, believers who endured long trials shared a common belief that God was doing something bigger than their current circumstances, something eternal that gave perspective to their earthly struggles. Paul reinforced this eternal view in the book of Ephesians. In Ephesians 1, 2, 3, and 6, he referred to all that is going on "in the heavens." Christ is seated in the heavens. We too are seated with him. And we are wrestling not against the wicked on earth but with the spiritual forces of evil in heavenly places. This truth will be reinforced when we read of Job in chapter seven.

Paul reminded the church in Ephesus that something was going on outside their line of vision in heaven, something that transcended their lifetime. Those transcendent truths informed their lives, and their lives in turn contributed to and reinforced the long story of God and his children from Genesis to Revelation. Focusing on the eternal doesn't diminish the value of our lives on earth but instills each moment of endurance with greater eternal value. This eternal perspective is the fuel for the hope that will not disappoint. But this perspective is only found through availing ourselves of our access to God's throne room through Christ, wherein we find the correct lenses to make sense of the rest of life.

Consider the changes to Asaph's perspective in Psalm 73:25-26.

Who do I have in heaven but you?
And I desire nothing on earth but you.
My flesh and my heart may fail,
but God is the strength of my heart,
my portion forever.

What do you desire on earth? To whom have you looked for rescue through your path of suffering? I desire the restoration of broken relationships and peace from physical suffering and have looked to pastors, counselors, and medical professionals again and again for help. Some things have helped, but many things I looked to have disappointed me greatly. When I enter the sanctuary of God and avail myself of the access to God that Christ's death provides, my desires get redirected to the only source that can ultimately reconcile all things. My flesh fails—I am physically overwhelmed. I am medically overwhelmed. My heart fails too—I am emotionally overwhelmed. I don't know how to navigate the burdens of broken relationships or the demoralization of ongoing ill health. But God is my strength and my portion forever.

Portion means our legacy or inheritance. In those days a parcel of land that was endowed to provide for an heir. God was Asaph's inheritance. In Christ, God is our inheritance, our portion, as well. He has endowed us with *himself* to provide for our deepest long-term needs, and our hope in him will not be disappointed.

In his letter to the church at Corinth, Paul gave insight into this portion, this inheritance, this endowment we receive through Christ: "God is able to make every grace overflow to you, so that in every way, always having everything you need, you may excel in every good work" (2 Corinthians 9:8).

Remember that grace and mercy we find in our time of need in the throne room of God (Hebrews 4:16)? Both Paul and the author of Hebrews teach that this grace is for our *need*. This endowment of grace is manifest to us particularly when we are at the end of our ropes. For it is at the end of our ropes, in our times of greatest need, that we are able to best see God's overflowing grace pouring into our lives.

I often visit St. Helena Sound on the South Carolina coast, where the Edisto River pours into the ocean. The pouring out of that one great body of water into a much bigger one is barely perceptible, the ending of the river indistinguishable from the beginning of the sea. In contrast, when a tropical storm dumped several inches of rain after months of drought on our farm, the difference was stark. The corn greened up and seemed to grow inches overnight. Grass that lay dormant for months suddenly needed to be mowed every few days. Our pond that was feet below normal quickly overflowed the spillway. Wealth and health do not keep someone from God's providential care. But for Asaph, and any sufferer who feels their feet slipping, the water of God's grace is especially poignant and effective when it comes in the drought of our deep need.

Charlie Dates, a pastor and seminary professor in Chicago, says it this way, "There is a kind of danger in power, a bit of slavery in wealth, and a latent misfortune in comfort. There must be, has to be real joy found somewhere else."[2] Asaph in Psalm 73 found something deep and sustaining not in spite of the suffering he experienced but because of it. It funneled him down to the sanctuary of God, for there was no refuge for him anywhere else. There, he found something deep and sustaining, something that abundantly blessed him and equipped him to endure with hope, something worth knowing.

> Those far from you will certainly perish;
>
> you destroy all who are unfaithful to you.
>
> But as for me, God's presence is my good.
>
> I have made the Lord God my refuge,
>
> so I can tell about all you do. (Psalm 73:27-28)

Asaph ends this chapter parked in God's throne room. The presence of God is his refuge. He hides there, mentally if not physically safe from the wicked who wear their pride like a necklace, who mock and threaten the righteous. He understands their condition apart from God now. He recognizes too that God's presence doesn't just bless him with good things but is itself his good. His theology is brutally and beautifully practical.

Asaph still has an honest understanding of the problems of his world. He ends the chapter with the correct perspective on the tension between those things we righteously long for and our current earthly reality. As you sit with Asaph in the tent of suffering, living in your own tension between your hopes and your reality, receive this cup of nourishing sustenance he offers. Asaph's tent of suffering turns out to be the sanctuary of God, where God provides us with himself as our rich supply. That changed everything in Asaph's perspective of the suffering in his life and community. God has provided himself in the same way for you. Rest in God's sanctuary for a bit, nourished by this truth.

REFLECT

What phrases from Psalm 73:1-16 reflect how you have felt during your own journey of suffering?

In what ways do you identify with Asaph's crisis of belief?

Hebrews 4:16 says that we can come boldly to God to receive help in our time of need. Have you made use of this access you have to God?

Have you felt that you needed to get yourself together before you cried out to God?

Read through Asaph's change of perspective in verses 18-28. Have you experienced such a change in perspective in the past? How would you describe it?

Asaph ends this psalm by saying he has made the Lord God his refuge. What do you think practically speaking that meant for Asaph?

What might that mean for you?

AMBIGUOUS LOSS

Fellowship in Exile

"I'm so sorry."

Those were the simple words the psychiatrist said to my friend Jenny in the lobby of the psychiatric ward where her husband had been admitted for the second time in four months. At Dave's first admission, doctors and Jenny thought his symptoms of confusion and hallucinations were from simple sleep deprivation. But after experiencing intense psychotic episodes a second time, it became clear that he had a much more serious, ongoing issue in his brain. He would eventually be diagnosed with schizoaffective disorder, and their lives would never be the same.[1]

As Jenny recounted her ongoing struggle to reconcile herself with Dave's diagnosis and the fundamental changes it brought in their home, I recognized in her a particular kind of grief. Dave was there, but the Dave she had fallen in love with years before seemed gone. Because he resisted treatment, he lived in a different version of reality than she and their children did. Day after day, week after week, month after month, the gulf grew between her understanding of reality and his. Though they still lived in the same house and shared the same bed, he experienced a different life in his head from the one she and her children experienced in their neighborhood and church.

Jenny mourned the loss of the man she had married, but it did not fit the normal stages of grief. Her grief was ongoing, and she was unable to put it to rest. The person she grieved was physically there, but mentally he seemed out of her reach. Because they no longer shared the same perceptions of reality, this fundamentally changed how Jenny could relate to or rely on Dave. There was no clear path for her grief to follow to mourn her loss. And each new day only rekindled her grief. Mourning the loss of the Dave she had known became the undercurrent of Jenny's life day in and day out, and she was unable to resolve it for years to come.

AMBIGUOUS LOSS

Over the last few decades, educator and researcher Pauline Boss has brought attention to the phrase *ambiguous loss*, which describes the ongoing grief associated with a person or thing that is both present and absent. Divorce, estrangement from children or parents, Alzheimer's, dementia, and traumatic brain injuries all result in ambiguous loss. The experience of a loved one sent to prison, deployed overseas, or missing in action also results in ambiguous loss. The loved one may still exist in your life, but they are not there in the way your relationship was experienced in the past or expected to be in the future. The impact of such losses are devastating, but the surrounding culture does not recognize them in the same way as other types of losses, and there are few cultural rituals to grieve such changes in life circumstances.[2] Those who experience such loss find it particularly alienating.

But once again, we are not left as orphans to navigate ambiguous loss on our own. In God's inspired revelation of himself to us, there are multiple examples of faithful believers experiencing ambiguous loss who can walk with us through our own. In 2 Samuel, David experienced such loss when his son Absalom rebelled against him and sought to take his throne. David both loved his son and feared his son. He wept as he ran from Absalom, exiled temporarily from the land, in fear of his own life (2 Samuel 15:30). Even as Absalom threatened David's right as king, David told his officers to spare Absalom's life in battle and mourned Absalom when he was killed, nearly to the expense of his own kingdom. David was torn between two sets of circumstances, the death of a son and the restoration of his kingdom, each evoking polar opposite emotions. Natural responses to both tangled together with no clear winner between them. Ambiguous, indeed.

Joseph experienced decades of ambiguous loss as well, recounted to us in Genesis 37–50. He was exiled from his family, without the ability to know of their welfare. We aren't given many clues to Joseph's emotional state during those years of loss in Egypt until his brothers show up looking for food. Then we read these poignant words: "Joseph hurried out because he was overcome with emotion for his brother, and he was about to weep. He went into an inner room and wept there" (Genesis 43:30). When Joseph finally revealed himself to his brothers, Scripture says, "Joseph could no longer keep his composure in front of all his attendants, so he called out, 'Send everyone away from me!' No one was with him when he revealed his identity to his brothers. But he wept so loudly that the Egyptians heard it, and also Pharaoh's household heard it" (Genesis 45:1-2).

Joseph had lived in agonizing tension for years, not knowing if his beloved father and little brother were dead or alive. He clearly had deep, pent-up emotions that he had hung onto for years, living in the unresolved tension of his circumstances of exile from those he most loved.

AN ALIENATED PROPHET

While Joseph alone was exiled in Egypt, alienated from his family and the life he had known as a child of Jacob, later in the history of Israel the entire nation was exiled. The southern tribes of Israel had disregarded God's law and ignored the warnings of the prophet Jeremiah. As a result of their rebellion against him, God's discipline was severe. They suffered as a result of their corporate disobedience. Yet, by all accounts, Jeremiah was a faithful prophet, warning the people exactly as God instructed. He too paid a price for their rebellion, exiled from his homeland and beloved Jerusalem. The book of Lamentations records Jeremiah's wrestling with God over this ongoing loss.[3]

In Lamentations 3:9, Jeremiah says, "[God] has walled in my ways with blocks of stone; he has made my paths crooked." Jenny identified well with the prophet's words. She had made covenant vows, "in sickness and in health," to Dave. She was walled in by her convictions on the sanctity of marriage. But suddenly the walled path had taken an unexpected turn, the way forward confusing. She had tried to make wise choices in her life, and up to that point in her marriage it seemed that God had made her paths straight in the way that Proverbs 3:5-6, a passage she loved, indicates. *Crooked* was the appropriate word for this strange new path she was navigating after the onset of Dave's psychiatric symptoms. She felt exiled from the life she had known and the person she had married.

The exile from Jerusalem to Babylon that walled Jeremiah on a crooked path was not the first time the children of Israel had been kept out of the Promised Land because of their disobedience. It was not the first time their wanderings had followed what seemed a crooked path. Centuries before, under the leadership of Moses, God worked many great miracles to free the Hebrews from their bondage in Egypt. Yet, despite God's demonstration of his power over Pharaoh through the plagues and parting of the Red Sea, ten of the twelve spies sent to scout out the Promised Land believed the men living in Canaan were too big for Israel to defeat.

In Numbers 14 the children of Israel threaten to overthrow Moses and find a leader to take them back to captivity in Egypt. Joshua and Caleb, the two faithful spies who were confident in God's ability to give them the land just as he said, tore their clothes. They were horrified at this turn in the story of their deliverance from Egypt and the gift of the Promised Land. After the straight path to the edge of the Promised Land from Egypt, they too were left in no-man's land to wander a very different, crooked path for forty years. Though it was not Joshua and Caleb's sin that walled them in on this new crooked path, they would wander with the rest of the nation, walled in by the sin of others, not their own.

DAILY BREAD FOR EXILES

In Joshua and Caleb's wandering in the wilderness, God demonstrated a great truth for anyone enduring the no-man's land of ambiguous loss. This lesson came through his gift of daily manna to his children walled in on a crooked path. This lesson was a gift to the ones who had caused the crooked path by their disobedience as much as those walled in by the wrong choices of others. The manna was literal food that physically sustained them. But the manna also became a figurative illustration of God's provision of Jesus, the Bread of Life, for any of us stuck on the crooked path of ambiguous loss.

The first lesson from God's provision of manna is seen in the instructions God gave for gathering it. In Exodus 16, God told Moses to instruct the Israelites to gather manna daily, storing extra only the morning before the Sabbath so they could rest weekly on that day set apart to worship God. Of course, the children of Israel tried to gather more than the allotted amount. Wouldn't we too? If there were a ton of bread on the ground or apples on the trees or corn on the stalks, wouldn't we gather as much as possible? Isn't the wise choice to take advantage of the resources of the day to plan for an unknown future? But when the Israelites attempted to gather more than the allotted daily amount, the manna quickly grew worms and stunk. Working hard to prepare for the future was not the lesson God had for them to learn. He instead, for forty years, trained the Israelites to depend on him daily. God didn't keep his children tied to him on a rope or a leash. He kept them on a keychain, as Beth Moore has put it. And when we are exiled from a loved one, caught in the crooked wandering of ambiguous loss, we are equally dependent on God for life-giving sustenance. Ambiguous loss that we can't reconcile keeps us utterly dependent on God, and that's not a bad thing.

In John 6, Jesus makes clear the fundamental second lesson from the Bible's use of manna in the long story of Scripture. After miraculously feeding a hungry multitude with physical loaves of bread, the crowd continued following Jesus. But they were clearly looking only for more free physical food, which led to this interaction between Jesus and the multitude.

> "What sign, then, are you going to do so we may see and believe you?" they asked. "What are you going to perform? Our ancestors ate the manna in the wilderness, just as it is written:
> **He gave them bread from heaven to eat.**"

Jesus said to them, "Truly I tell you, Moses didn't give you the bread from heaven, but my Father gives you the true bread from heaven. For the bread of God is the one who comes down from heaven and gives life to the world."

Then they said, "Sir, give us this bread always."

"I am the bread of life," Jesus told them. "No one who comes to me will ever be hungry, and no one who believes in me will ever be thirsty again." (John 6:32-35)

This wasn't the answer the crowd following Jesus wanted to hear, but it is the answer anyone exiled in ambiguous loss desperately needs today. Jesus is the Bread of Life we need *daily* to sustain us along the walled in, crooked path we walk.

JESUS SAVES AND SANCTIFIES

At the final plague before the exodus from Egypt, God gave Israel a clear picture of Jesus' coming work to cleanse them and us of our guilt so the wrath of God would pass over us. The blood of the Passover lamb painted on the lintel and the doorpost of Israelite homes caused the angel of death to pass over those homes, protecting Israelite firstborn children from God's wrath against unbelieving Egyptians. It modeled Jesus' role in our justification, his blood shed for us that caused God's wrath to pass over us.

God's gift of daily manna, given less than a year after the initial Passover, modeled for the Israelites Jesus' coming role in their sanctification, their daily walk after salvation as they continued in faith and grew in holiness. *Sanctification* is the theological term for the process of believers becoming in reality what God has already declared them to be at their justification—righteous as Christ is righteous. The Israelites needed daily nourishment to persevere against sin and trial because weekly or monthly nourishment wouldn't last. They couldn't collect a week's worth of manna on a given day. This was the fundamental lesson of manna for them and us. We need the spiritual nourishment of the Bread of Life anew each day, and we are daily dependent on God for the next provision. This is how God changes us and sets us apart to do his work, that is, how he sanctifies us.

This truth vexed me as the finalizing of my divorce approached on the calendar and again as the same feelings of loss followed me after the date passed. It vexed me as I prepared to move my boys and myself back to our family farm and the support of my parents and sisters after my divorce. It vexed me as I packed up my home in my well-loved neighborhood of Seattle. And it vexed me through the repeating cycles of surgery and recovery, surgery and recovery, surgery and recovery I experienced after I moved back.

I didn't want to be utterly dependent on nourishment from God day by day, hour by hour. I wanted to stock up on faith and confidence, on joy and peace, and I wanted that stockpile to last me for a while. I wanted to shop for God's provisions at Costco, not a food truck. But whatever peace or hope I found on any given day seemed to be eaten by worms within twenty-four hours. I reached the end of myself every day, sometimes twice a day. I felt guilt for the fleeting nature of my hope and joy. When I found encouragement, why couldn't I hang on to it for an extended period of time? What was wrong with me?

But over time, I learned the lesson of daily manna, which is also the lesson of the Lord's Prayer for daily bread in the Gospels. God does not want a monthly or weekly relationship with me. He does not allow me to stock up on spiritual nourishment like I am shopping at Costco. He wants a daily relationship. He wants an hourly one. I need him like a food truck, getting enough for one meal and returning for the next. I am not his adult child calling occasionally from college when I need money. I am his toddler child, dependent on him throughout the day for food and dress, for the most basic necessities of my spiritual, emotional, and physical life. Though I want to be independent and somewhat strong on my own, my losses and ongoing needs have exposed that I am a very needy child of God. But I no longer feel guilt that I need the same lessons and the same provision over and over in my walk. No, that is exactly as God intends. The stresses and losses associated with exile from a land or loved one you formerly relied on are the places where this daily need for God is exposed. For me, this has been a good thing.

I have spent most of the years of my ambiguous loss, my exile, in churches that practice the ordinance of Communion weekly. In Matthew 26:26, Jesus took the bread at the table as he and the disciples ate their last Passover meal together, blessed it, and gave it to the disciples with these words: "Take and eat it; this is my body." When I eat the bread weekly with other believers in my church, I think of the spiritual nourishment from Jesus that it symbolizes. The bread represents his body that was broken for me, and by his wounds I am healed. The wine represents his blood that was shed for me. It is painted on my doorposts, causing God's wrath to pass over me. There is no condemnation on me for my past, even if I did sinfully contribute to my own exile. I confess my sins, for Jesus' punishment has paid the price and bought my peace. Jesus is the bread and the blood that sustains me.

The reminder of all Christ has done for me through weekly Communion ministers great grace to me. But it doesn't free me of daily need throughout the week. I often catch myself withering midweek with weakened faith and fears for the future. I have learned to examine myself, *When was the last time I spent time reading Scripture and praying to God?* Without exception, I realize that I became busy with the responsibilities of life and for days haven't sat quietly with the Lord reading the Bible. The answer to my withering hope or joy is always for me to find a quiet place where I can read Scripture and pray without interruption. And when I am too weak to lift the spoon of spiritual nourishment to my own mouth, I have believing friends who speak it to me patiently, some multiple times a week. When I have been unable to get to my church for corporate worship for an extended period of time, some of them have come to me. I cannot survive exile without consistent nourishment from the Bread of Life. You can't survive the wilderness without manna.

REBUILDING

In the end Joshua and Caleb survived forty years walled in on a crooked path through the wilderness, sustained by daily bread from the ground each morning. Then the Lord freed them from their crooked path in miraculous ways and brought them into the Promised Land with great triumph. The book of Joshua is an encouraging recount of God's faithfulness through it all.

In contrast, most historians believe that Jeremiah died in Egypt in exile. He did not get to return to Jerusalem and see to the rebuilding of the walls of the city and the temple that Ezra and Nehemiah later led. But God showed Jeremiah the coming restoration from afar and instructed Jeremiah to write words that God would fulfill less than a generation later.

> As for you, my servant Jacob,
> do not be afraid—
>   this is the Lord's declaration—
> and do not be discouraged, Israel,
> for without fail I will save you out of a distant place,
> your descendants, from the land of their captivity!
> Jacob will return and have calm and quiet
> with no one to frighten him. . . .
> I will bring you health
> and will heal you of your wounds. (Jeremiah 30:10, 17)

In the next chapter Jeremiah prophesied that God would "build you so that you will be rebuilt" (Jeremiah 31:4). It's funny language, but I get the point. God would build anew what had been razed at their exile, but it would be a restorative building, a righting of wrongs, restoring what had been destroyed.

If you are in a long season of ambiguous loss, you are not alone in your exile. Scripture guides you through your lament, but it also gives us hope for the restoration of things that seem lost in the ether, the rebuilding of things totally destroyed.

> You will take up your tambourines again
> and go out in joyful dancing.
> You will plant vineyards again
> on the mountains of Samaria;
>   the planters will plant and will enjoy the fruit.
>   (Jeremiah 31:4-5)

A day is coming when you will pick up your tambourine and dance for joy, unencumbered by the weights of your losses. It may be in this life. It surely will be in the life to come. Of that day, C. S. Lewis gives us sweet insight in *The Last Battle,* my favorite of his books. "All their life in this world and all their adventures in Narnia had only been the cover and the title page: now at last they were beginning Chapter One of the Great Story which no one on earth has read: which goes on for ever: in which every chapter is better than the one before."[4]

In the meantime, feast daily on Jesus, the Bread of Life, because he alone sustains you as you wait on God to build what needs to be rebuilt in your life. "I am the vine, you are the branches; he who abides in Me and I in him, he bears much fruit, for apart from Me you can do nothing" (John 15:5 NASB).

REFLECT

Ambiguous loss describes the path of grief associated with mourning a person or thing that is both present and absent. How have you experienced ambiguous loss?

This chapter referenced several biblical examples of ambiguous loss: David in his conflict with his son Absalom; Joseph exiled in Egypt away from his family; Joshua and Caleb longing to enter the Promised Land but stuck for forty years wandering the wilderness; and Jeremiah walled in on a crooked path by the disobedience of the people to whom he prophesied. Do you see parallels between your path of suffering and any of theirs?

What lessons do you glean from God's provision of daily manna for Joshua, Caleb, Moses, and the other children of Israel wandering the wilderness for forty years?

How is this manna symbolic of the provision God has given us through Jesus?

LEARNING TO LAMENT

Fellowship with Job

The weekend I wrestled the news out of the nurse that my biopsy came back showing cancer, everything in my life changed. All of my plans put themselves on hold. Enrollment was down at the community college where I taught part-time, so my classes were canceled, and I was out of a job. I had volunteered at my children's school on my days off, but I could not bring myself to even darken the doors as they returned to school while I waited on my surgery date. I stopped going to Sunday school and stepped back from leading women's midweek Bible study. I quit mid project a proposal I was working on for a book, and I never returned to it.

During those early weeks, I could not think about any but the most basic details of life. If it took more thought than putting on yoga pants or baking a frozen pizza, it was beyond me. To think about any detail of my life meant opening myself up to all of them: my situation as a single mom of two middle school boys, supporting myself with part-time income, facing invasive surgeries with extensive recovery times, possibly months of chemotherapy and radiation, unsure of the stage of my cancer and my prognosis for recovery. All without a spouse to shoulder the load.

The youngest of three daughters, I had long had an independent streak, traipsing halfway across the country to work at a summer camp during my college years and living internationally for a year after college graduation. After my marriage, I moved from the East Coast, and the only state where several generations of my family had lived, to Seattle, Washington, enjoying the adventure that came with moving to the unknown. But with my marriage I allowed my independent self to become financially, emotionally, and even spiritually dependent on another. Divorce felt like an amputation of a limb I depended on daily, and afterwards I felt the strong need to find my own way forward again, independently. I wanted to build a new life with safeguards so no one could ever sabotage it again. That wasn't a realistic desire, but it was my coping mechanism nonetheless.

I had been at the end of my rope after the divorce, just barely beginning to claw my way back to some semblance of self-sufficiency and emotional stability after I moved back home to the safety net of family on the East Coast. Now, with this cancer diagnosis, I hadn't just lost any ground I had gained; I felt in a full free fall. I couldn't get my bearings. I couldn't feel a rope to hang on to, even if I was at its end.

During the weeks between the first call that I had cancer and my mastectomy to remove it, I knew what I needed to read in Scripture—the story of Job. But reading Scripture in the midst of deep grief often seemed impossible. When physically able, I found listening to the Bible on audio through the Christian Standard Bible app a great help as I walked the familiar loop around my house over and over again. When physically unable to walk, I found coloring an adult coloring book of verses sent to me by a friend a great help to my mind as well.

I'd read Job before. I'd written about Job before. I knew the nuts and bolts of his story and the theology of suffering it teaches. But I couldn't bring myself to start it. It took me weeks from first thinking I needed to sit in Job's story to actually attempting to read it.

I liked the book of Job better as a help for someone else who was suffering, offering me encouragement that I could then offer them. I did not like being able to identify personally with Job, particularly in the piling of serious trial upon serious trial, each with their own deep weights of grief.

I also knew what came at the end of the book of Job, and I wasn't ready to face that yet. I was still wrestling with feelings of betrayal by God for allowing this unexpected diagnosis on top of the suffering my children and I were already experiencing in the wake of losing our friends and family life in Seattle. In the final chapters of Job, God speaks firmly to him, and Job submitted to God. I wasn't there yet, but Job was exactly the companion I needed to get to that point, which is the miracle of God's grace and mercy through his Word. I needed to fellowship with Job in his tent. I needed to hear the words of his own struggle. I needed him as a guide as I walked through my own suffering. He can be a helpful companion to you too.

Once I finally made myself listen to the deep-voiced reader of Job on my audio Bible app, I was struck by how long the lament and questions of suffering went on between Job and his friends before God broke in to set things straight. I spent the weeks between my diagnosis and first surgery listening to Job's lament as I walked the dirt loop around my farmhouse. I listened slowly, sometimes repeating chapters where Job talked, though I mostly skipped those where his friends lectured with their faulty understanding of God and humans. I didn't reach God's strong words to Job at the end of the book until a while after my mastectomy. Job's long lament ended up being exactly what I needed to come to terms with what God allowed in my life and his right to do so.

Job's lament became mine for the weeks before my first surgery. He was my comrade as I cried out to God. When friend after friend shared with me that my diagnosis caused them to struggle with their faith as much as it did me, Job gave me words to put to my wrestling. Why did God allow this diagnosis on top of the previous weight of struggle from the collapse of my family as I knew it? Thankfully, God had not left me as an orphan with my deep, dark emotions.

PULLING BACK THE CURTAIN

My boys enjoy video games that have them going on a quest with other online players. The first goal when a new round begins is to gather tools and weapons. Players drop into a field or arena and look for food, first-aid kits, or weapons. In one iteration of a recent game, they were happy to find a shopping cart. I found it funny, but it helped them carry their food and weapons, so it had some purpose in the game.

The first two chapters of Job are a treasure trove of essential gear and weapons for a believer entering an arena of severe trial upon trial. We are wise to gather up all the help those chapters offer to put into our figurative shopping cart wherever the path of our suffering takes us. We need these truths with us at all times in the arena of suffering, ready to pull out when Satan tempts us to despair.

The first chapter of Job begins by pulling back the curtain in the heavens on a discussion occurring between God and Satan. From that discussion I gathered my first weapon against the prosperity gospel that sufferers must put to death. It is a nugget of sustaining truth every believing sufferer needs to know: *You did not bring this on yourself.*

The prosperity gospel teaches that health, wealth, and good fortune follow Christians who make good choices. But the opening words of the book of Job tell us that Job was a righteous man of integrity. In fact, Job's faithfulness drew Satan to challenge God, "Job only obeys you because you bless him." Satan accused God of the prosperity gospel! God set Satan right, though. True worshipers worship God because God is worthy of worship, not because God promises a one-to-one correlation of rewards for obedient acts. This affirmation in the heavens of Job's faithfulness was out of Job's line of sight. Though we see behind the curtain, Job never did. The fact that Job knew none of this provided the very framework that proved Satan wrong.

In these opening chapters I found deep sustenance for facing my early bewilderment with my diagnosis. Why was this happening to me? What had I done to bring this on myself? Why was I facing another devastating trial when I was still in the middle of the previous one? I felt God had turned his back on me, so surely I deserved it. My pastors had walked closely with me through my divorce in an effort to help me avoid it, and I knew in their opinion I had not brought that on myself. Yet I struggled with these thoughts, eventually seeing a Christian counselor who spoke truth to me when I couldn't see it for myself.

As the weeks turned into months and the months into years, I eventually accepted both my divorce and my cancer, and I have had enough counsel from brothers and sisters in Christ I trust to confront me when I sin to no longer believe I brought either my divorce or my cancer on myself. These trusted friends, the hands and feet of Jesus, have spoken God's counsel clearly to me and helped me see truths I couldn't see in the fog of suffering on my own. But when I was still reeling with questions from both my divorce and my cancer, and not thinking logically about either, God ministered much grace to me by allowing me to see behind the curtain of Job's suffering, though I couldn't yet see behind the curtain of my own. Friends speaking this truth to me was important. But when God, my eternal authority, spoke this truth to me through the story of Job, that made the final difference in my ability to believe it for myself. The question wasn't whether Job was a righteous man. The question was if God's worthiness to be worshiped stemmed from more than his physical gifts to his children.

God is worthy to be worshiped even when the curtain obscures our sight of his goodness or his purposes.

WHEN THE NUMBNESS WEARS OFF

We are not given the time frame for the length between the first round of attack on Job's family in chapter 1 and the second round of attack on Job's own body in chapter 2. But eventually, the numbness wears off and Job gives language to his misery in chapter 3. We get to sit with Job in his own tent of suffering and lament with him as he in turn gives us language to lament for ourselves.

Job began by cursing the day of his birth.

Why is light given to one burdened with grief,
    and life to those whose existence is bitter,
    who wait for death, but it does not come,

and search for it more than for hidden treasure? . . .

For the thing I feared has overtaken me,

and what I dreaded has happened to me.

I cannot relax or be calm;

I have no rest, for turmoil has come. (Job 3:20-21, 25-26)

I'm not sure if Job is praying to God, talking to his friends, or just verbalizing his grief to no one in particular. My lament has taken all those forms, sometimes all within a few minutes. Job has lost, for the time being, all sense of hope. He desires death as a welcome relief to the pain of his life. He is anxious, unable to rest. He feels that there is no balm for his soul.

The thing Job feared and dreaded had overtaken him. I too remember the fear I experienced when a faithful Christian friend went through a divorce, years before my own. So help me, I did not want to experience that! But I thought my marriage was solid. My husband and I worshiped God together and seemed true partners in every sense of the word. I took seriously the things I thought I needed to do to "guard my marriage." In the end, the thing I most feared, the destruction of my home as I knew it, overtook me, and I couldn't find a way to release its grip on me.

Afterwards, I worked to figure out my path forward, to find secure footing for my children and myself on a foundation that no man could snatch from under me again. Yet, here I was, a second unspoken fear overtaking me with the diagnosis of cancer, my fear of losing independence and control of my life because of my health.

Job's words ministered much grace to me. I was not alone in the antsy anxiety I felt, like a caged animal who couldn't find a way out of the bars these trials had put around my life. What a sweet blessing to my anxious, pacing self to know another who felt the same anxiety, who paced long before I was ever born, his pacing recorded in the eternal words of Scripture *without condemnation*.

This was helpful to me during the weeks of reading Job's lament in the lead up to my first surgery. In all these things Job did not sin, the early chapters record. And from studying the book at other times, I knew the ending chapters contained a similar affirmation of the character of Job.

> After the LORD had finished speaking to Job, he said to Eliphaz the Temanite: "I am angry with you and your two friends, for you have not spoken the truth about me, as my servant Job has. Now take seven bulls and seven rams, go to my servant Job, and offer a burnt offering for yourselves. Then my servant Job will pray for you. I will surely accept his prayer and not deal with you as your folly deserves. For you have not spoken the truth about me, as my servant Job has." (Job 42:7-8)

After Job's gut-wrenching questions of God and bitter lament, the Scripture says God *answered* him. God answered and corrected Job, but he was angry with only Job's friends. The difference in answering and correcting versus angry rebuke is important. God's answer to Job was strong and definitive, and we will deal with it and Job's response to it in chapter 8. But when God roused himself in strong defense of his glory, power, and righteousness in all of these things to Job, he did not condemn Job for his lament and questions. He corrected him, but he did not condemn him.

Sufferers who have been believers for any length of time know from their time in church that our Christian faith calls us to believe God is all-powerful, all-knowing, and very good. Our Christian faith teaches us to *trust* and *obey* God. Though I mostly outwardly obeyed God in the weeks of coming to terms with my diagnosis, I struggled greatly to trust. I couldn't immediately get from the circumstances newly dumped in my lap to the trust I knew I was supposed to have in my God. But as I sat in Job's tent, he gave me thirty-seven chapters of wrestling with God. It was a great gift to me. I don't know how long this discussion went on between Job and his friends before God finally spoke in Job 38, but the time it took me to read through those chapters helped me get to the place where I could hear from God when he finally spoke to Job from the whirlwind and submit to him in my own suffering.

WHY?

In those thirty-seven chapters, Job verbalized the question *why* from many different angles. He began with a why question I have asked often, "Why even bother?" He says in Job 7:1-4 that he is like a hired servant with no control over his own existence. His only allotment is months of vanity and nights of trouble. What was the point of any righteous, responsible choice he had made up to this point in his life if it could all be taken away in an instant? All was emptiness. He had lost hope of ever seeing good again (Job 7:7).

Unlike the psalmist of Psalm 73, who struggled in his heart but worked not to verbalize it and deny God, Job gave full vent to his struggle in Job 7:11.

Therefore I will not restrain my mouth.
I will speak in the anguish of my spirit;
I will complain in the bitterness of my soul.

Job gave full vent to the anguish in his spirit, and I found that I had to do the same. I couldn't toe the line of what I thought a good Christian sufferer should say and do. But I have come to realize now that is the entire point of the book of Job. Suffering exposed both my weakness and Job's. It exposed our utter need for God. I could not maintain my trust in God on my own. And though Job had done well in the early days of his trials, his trust in God was weak by Job 7 as well.

From utter hopelessness at the vanity of life, Job turned his questions of why directly to God.

> If I have sinned, what have I done to you,
> Watcher of humanity?
> Why have you made me your target,
> so that I have become a burden to you? (Job 7:20)

This question leads Job to examine the prosperity gospel he had believed. By Job 9 he seems to have put that false gospel away. "[God] destroys both the blameless and the wicked" (Job 9:22). There is no one-to-one correlation between righteous acts and material blessing. The answer to poverty isn't to give more money to God. The answer to sickness isn't to sacrifice more. Job is right to put away this false gospel, this works-based righteousness. But it doesn't solve Job's wrestling with the question of why. It only opened the door to a deeper place of wrestling, questions we inevitably must face in our journey of deep suffering once the prosperity gospel wears off. What's the point then of righteousness and faith? If it doesn't bring the promise of material blessing or protection from suffering in this life, how is it not vanity too? The book of Job sits in that question a long time without immediately answering it.

In chapter 10, Job gives voice to the wretched pit in which he sits.

> Are my days not few? Stop it!
> Leave me alone, so that I can smile a little

before I go to a land of darkness and gloom,

never to return.

It is a land of blackness like the deepest darkness,

gloomy and chaotic,

where even the light is like the darkness. (Job 10:20-22)

What dark, depressing words Job utters. "Stop it, God! Leave me alone, and maybe I can have a few smiles before the darkness over-takes me for good." I cry as I write these words, for I have felt the same. Leave me alone, God, and maybe I can make a little peace for me and my children on my own.

Like the true Father he is, God had been my Comforter from youth, his Word ministering to me at hard turns in life in middle school, high school, and college. When I felt rejected by a boy-friend in college, Jesus was the lover of my soul, my Bridegroom who would never leave me or forsake me. The Godhead had com-forted me when diagnosed with diabetes as a lay missionary in South Korea, and when I miscarried my first child, God held me by the hand as he did the psalmist in Psalm 73.

But here I was now wishing God would just leave me alone.

I had no other place to take my deep, dark questions of God but to God himself. When I read Job saying the same things I was feeling internally, God ministered great grace to me.

THE OLDEST STORY

Bible historians believe that Job's story was the first written of Scripture. After the fall, the oldest written piece of God's revelation was about this sufferer proving to Satan God's worthiness to be worshiped simply on his own merits. How long after the loss of Eden did Job live? Did he grow up hearing stories passed down by generations of the beauty and peace of Eden tragically lost by the sin of Adam and Eve? His story reflects all that was lost in the fall, his children killed, his wealth destroyed, his body sickened, his relationships marred.

As I listened to Job, walking the dirt loop around my house, coming to terms with my diagnosis of breast cancer, the implications that God chose to put Job's account on paper first were not lost on me. This first writing is a story firmly set in the death and destruction of life after the fall. It is a story that puts to death the prosperity gospel and points us toward different, better good news. The first story is about a man learning that his relationship with God wasn't transactional or performance based. The first story is about him coming to understand that God is much greater than we can fathom. And it is about him looking for someone to stand between him and God, knowing that he could not stand on his own.

The New American Standard Bible provides this header for Job 9: "Job says there is no arbitrator between God and man." That summary is the underlying framework for Job's struggle chapter after chapter, but particularly for chapter 9. How can I be right before God? Job wonders (Job 9:1). God is not a man Job can take to court (Job 9:32). There is no umpire that can settle matters between God and Job (Job 9:33), for Job cannot stand alone before God. As Psalm 130:3 articulates, "LORD, if you kept an account of iniquities, Lord, who could stand?" Suffering exposed Job's utter need before God. Job's righteousness wasn't enough.

As Job's wrestling and lament continues, we get to his words in Job 19, from which many a Christian hymn and praise chorus have been written. With these words, we get another essential weapon for enduring suffering with hope.

But I know that my Redeemer lives,

and at the end he will stand on the dust.

Even after my skin has been destroyed,

yet I will see God in my flesh.

I will see him myself;

my eyes will look at him, and not as a stranger.

My heart longs within me. (Job 19:25-27)

Job, surrounded by the heinous effects of the fall, knew he needed someone else to change his position before God and enable him to stand before him. Though Job didn't yet know the name Jesus or Messiah, he believed one lived who would do just that. A Redeemer lived, one who would stand where Job could not, one who would allow Job to see God face-to-face. In the midst of Job's continued lament, we see the first true glimpses of hope. "I will see God," Job says, "and when I see him, he won't be a stranger." With the whole revelation of God, we now understand this is fulfilled in Christ. As Paul writes in Ephesians 2:19, "You are no longer foreigners and strangers, but fellow citizens with the saints, and members of God's household." God is no stranger to those who believe in Christ.

In grace our Father in heaven eternally preserved the story of Job for all who suffer in Christ today. God truly has not left us as orphans to walk our path of suffering alone. As we sit with Job in his tent of suffering and listen to his lament, we are freed from the dangerously deceptive heresy of the prosperity gospel that has us worshiping the gifts rather than the Giver. Job helps free us from the demoralizing questions we face in our own suffering—like "what did I do to deserve this?" Job was a righteous man, and his suffering wasn't because of his sin but to show the worthiness of God to Satan and the heavenly realm. Furthermore, Job rightly lamented his losses before God, and the Scriptures affirm multiple times that he did not sin in doing so.

In a book on companionship in suffering, it might feel natural to focus on Job's friends who came to Job at the end of chapter 2 to "sympathize with him and comfort him" (Job 2:11). But instead of using the relationship between Job and his friends as a lesson in what is and is not healthy community in suffering, I hope that you, like me, will find in Job himself a friend who gives permission to voice your deep struggles with God, first in lament of what God has allowed in your life and then in hope of the Redeemer who stands perfectly in your place.

Spend time reading the many chapters of Job's lament (or listening to them on audio if reading them feels beyond you). Never read the final chapters of Job without sitting with him as he laments in the first thirty-seven. Job is your companion in voicing your own lament to God, and the power of the conclusion of Job is built on the long lament that precedes it.

REFLECT

In Job 1:1-12 Satan brings accusations about both Job (and God himself) to God. What strikes you about this conversation between God and Satan?

In Job 3:20-26, Job cries out in despair. When we are at a loss for how to pray or respond to grievous things in our lives, Scripture leaves us an example. How does Job's lament help you put words to your own grief?

Job lays out his complaint before God in many chapters, but in Job 29–31, he makes his argument and frustration crystal clear. In response to his friends' faulty theology that he must have brought this on himself by his own sin, Job recounts in chapter 29 his righteousness and the subsequent respect he experienced in the land. In chapter 31, he argues his righteousness throughout the various relationships he had in life. Why do you think he spent so long attempting to prove his righteousness?

Have you felt a similar need to self justify around others?

In chapter 30 Job turns from recounting the respect he had in his community to lamenting how those around him view him now. He describes being despised by those younger than him. Like many of us, he feels like a pariah. How are sufferers sometimes despised by others around them?

Have you felt like a pariah?

Do you fear others despising you in the future?

FINDING REST

Deeper Fellowship with Job

8

During my mastectomy, they found cancer in one lymph node, which complicated my prognosis going forward. Cancer in one lymph node wasn't horrible. But it wasn't good either. I had prayed hard before my surgery that we caught it before it was in a lymph node because I understood that my treatment options and long-term prognosis were affected greatly by that one indicator. But the cancer had escaped my breast, and my oncologist scheduled me for six months of intense chemotherapy to kill the cancer cells that might be floating around my body, potentially settling in my lungs or brain. I was a single parent in my forties with two middle school-age children. In the oncologist's opinion, we couldn't risk not doing it. But I couldn't imagine enduring it for six months either.

Two days before I was scheduled to begin chemotherapy, a CT scan showed a massive tumor in my abdomen. After multiple conversations with my breast surgeon and oncologist, they transferred me to a specialist at the Medical University of South Carolina because this type of tumor was rare and out of their area of expertise. If I had been scared at my original cancer diagnosis, I was terrified now. My pastor later shared with me that he and his wife had been terrified for me too.

Doctors suspected the new tumor was a liposarcoma, a type of cancer with a much higher rate of recurrence and death than my original breast cancer. I read the reports from the doctors after the CT scan and looked up all of the types of tumor it could potentially be. As I waited the two weeks it took to get in with the new surgeon, I continued listening to Job.

COUNTERINTUITIVE WORDS OF COMFORT

During this agitated waiting period, as I paced, wrestled, threw things, and cried out to God, I reached the moment in Job's story when God finally spoke to Job, a moment that disturbed me greatly when I first read it years before. The longer I've suffered though, the more I realize the essential necessity of this moment between any who suffer and the God they place their faith in. I experienced this moment as Job did, and it was the doorway through which I finally found rest.

Job had lost all of his children, lost all of his financial resources, and was covered in painful boils. Everything he had invested his life in had become dust. His comforters didn't bring him comfort. In his bitter complaint, he cried that he didn't even know where to look for God. His lament peppered with his friends' ill comfort lasted for thirty-seven chapters in the book of Job.

Job was a righteous man by God's own account, and he was not in this miserable place by his own foolishness. If anyone deserved true comfort, by my system of accounting, it was Job. After God's long silence during Job's lament and the sorry responses of his friends, God finally spoke in chapter 38. But God's words to Job do not fit the profile of what I think Job deserved to hear.

Then the LORD answered Job from the whirlwind. He said:
> Who is this who obscures my counsel
> with ignorant words?
> Get ready to answer me like a man;
> when I question you, you will inform me.
> Where were you when I established the earth?
> Tell me, if you have understanding.
> Who fixed its dimensions? Certainly you know!
> Who stretched a measuring line across it?
> What supports its foundations?
> Or who laid its cornerstone
> while the morning stars sang together
> and all the sons of God shouted for joy? (Job 38:1-7)

God continued on this way for four chapters. "I am *God*, Job! I hung the stars in the sky, created the oceans and every animal in them. Can you do that? I am all-powerful and all-knowing. Don't act as if you could possibly know better on any issue than I do."

When I first read this, I was taken aback. I expected God to say something more comforting to Job, at least as I define comfort. I know many passages of comfort elsewhere in Scripture that seem much more appropriate for this moment with Job.

- Nothing can separate us from the love of God.

- God works all things together for our good.

- They who wait on God mount up on wings like eagles.

- He who began the good work in us will be faithful to complete it.

But God said nothing like this in his answer to Job. Instead, to the guy who was at the lowest point of anyone ever named in Scripture,

God said, "I am God. I am all powerful. And I know what I'm doing!"

As I listened to God's response to Job in chapter 38, I remember being struck by verses 31-35.

> Can you fasten the chains of the Pleiades
> or loosen the belt of Orion?
> Can you bring out the constellations in their season
> and lead the Bear and her cubs?
> Do you know the laws of heaven?
> Can you impose its authority on earth?
> Can you command the clouds
> so that a flood of water covers you?
> Can you send out lightning bolts, and they go?
> Do they report to you: "Here we are"? (Job 38:31-35)

My faith says that God created our world and hung the stars in the sky. As a college math instructor, I am familiar with the physics of planetary motion, but only enough to wonder at the complex science that keeps them orbiting the sun in our solar system. I understand only the very tip of the iceberg when it comes to the laws of the constellations.

A thought started to settle in my psyche. Maybe God was doing similar things in my own life, holding my life and my children's lives in his hands as he holds the constellations. Maybe the fact that I don't understand what he is allowing in my life should not challenge my faith any more than the fact I don't understand fully how the earth I'm standing on maintains its rotation around the sun. Maybe I could trust God with my life as I trust him to hold the solar system together. Maybe I didn't need to fear the outcome of this second surgery any more than

I needed to fear a meteor would knock the earth out of orbit that night as I slept.

The wonderful thing at night on a farm is the lack of city lights obscuring the stars. On a clear night I can see Venus and Mars, sometimes even Jupiter and Saturn. I was recovered enough from the first surgery, waiting for the second, to walk the loop around my farmhouse again, this time at night—staring at the stars. I contemplated both their majesty and the fact that I didn't understand what exactly kept them hanging in the sky. When I saw Orion's Belt, I remembered God's words, "Can you loosen Orion's Belt, Wendy?" "No, God," I had to humbly respond. "I cannot."

As I stared at the night sky in that season, feeling the weight of the tumor in my abdomen as I walked, I recognized that though I had no control over the place of the stars in the evening skies, they remained there consistently nonetheless by greater laws than I understood. The fact that I didn't understand what was happening with Orion's Belt did not mean that something real and good wasn't at work holding it in the sky. The same was true of the path of my life, complicated further by finding this new tumor. The fact that I didn't understand what was happening and couldn't see the path forward didn't mean that God wasn't doing good things in and for me through it. Those nightly walks staring at the sky soothed my soul and pointed me to these truths. Now it wasn't just Job who accompanied me in my suffering, but God himself was answering me now too.

NECESSARY FAITH

As I read the end of Job leading up to my second surgery, I noted that this wasn't the first time God had comforted me with words counter-intuitive to those I thought I needed when suffering. Years before, when wrestling through the multiple trials of dear family and friends that weighed deeply on me, I cried out for God to speak to me and direct me: "God, give me something to make sense of this time in life. Help me know how to think about these hard circumstances and how to respond in obedience." I don't know what I expected, but God's words from my regular Scripture reading were pretty clear in the coming days, "Without faith it is impossible to please God" (Hebrews 11:6). I know from the rest of that verse exactly what God meant by faith that pleases him: "the one who draws near to him must believe that he exists and that he rewards those who seek him."

God didn't tell me that my troubles would soon end or that things would make more sense in time. Instead, he said pretty clearly through Scripture, "Trust Me! Believe that I exist, and believe that I am good to my children. I know what I am doing."

This trust God calls sufferers to is only seen or known in the context of situations when we do not understand what he is doing. God never explained to Job (at least according to the scriptural account) the purpose for his suffering. As far as we know, Job didn't know until heaven what was going on behind the curtain between God and Satan. In fact, Job's suffering seemed to have no earthly purpose at all during Job's lifetime. It was fully about proving the trustworthiness of God's character in the heavenly places to Satan and his minions. But during God's long silence, Job lamented to God, sustained by the truth that his Redeemer lived and would enable him to stand before God, known by God.

Satan couldn't believe Job would trust God based simply on God's character and not on the blessings on earth he gives us. *But those with true faith do not worship God because God is good but because God is God.* The faithful don't endure suffering because they expect deliverance but because God is worthy. I couldn't fully clarify this in my heart until God stopped fitting my definition of goodness and required me to sit patiently at his feet with unanswered prayers for a long season. Even if that season of unanswered prayer lasts the remainder of my life, my faith says that God is still good and still worthy of my praise.

JOB TURNS IN GOD'S ARMS

For four chapters God corrected all that had been misattributed to him concerning his sovereignty and goodness. He went on about the stars and the seas, birds and sea creatures, and oddly enough, mountain goats. For some reason, God's questions about mountain goats stuck with me, and I began contemplating all I did not know or have control over about mountain goats along with all I did not understand about the solar system.

> Job then replied to God,
> I know that you can do anything
> and no plan of yours can be thwarted.
> You asked, "Who is this who conceals my counsel with
>   ignorance?"
> Surely I spoke about things I did not understand,
> things too wondrous for me to know.
> You said, "Listen now, and I will speak.
> When I question you, you will inform me."
> I had heard reports about you,
> but now my eyes have seen you.
> Therefore, I reject my words and am sorry for them;
> I am dust and ashes. (Job 42:2-6)

In Job's response we see deep reverential awe and fear of God. Proverbs 1:7 says that the fear of the Lord is the beginning of knowledge. Job bowed his knee to God in light of God's awesome power and knowledge. This is a turning point for him. Proverbs 1:7 also says that fools despise wisdom and discipline. Though we often confuse the concepts of punishment and discipline, discipline is distinctly different from punishment. It means training in right-eousness. Job would have been a fool to despise the wisdom and training in righteousness that God spoke in the previous four chapters, and Job was no fool.

My contemplation of mountain goats and solar systems fun-neled me down to a similar response to God. For all who suffer there comes a moment in our wrestling with God when we too must tremble under God's awesome majesty, though we are faced with an insurmountable wall of unanswered questions, as was Job. If you are personally suffering right now, you could never hear such an exhortation to submit to God from someone who had not suf-fered intently. I certainly could not. But I could hear it from Job. Job earned his right to sit across the table from me in my tent of suffering and tell me I needed to submit to God. That submitting to God and believing in his power and goodness was the doorway to peace and rest.

Remember how Paul described the fellowship of suffering in Philippians 3:12? "Not that I have already reached the goal or am already perfect, but I make every effort to take hold of it because I also have been taken hold of by Christ Jesus." Christ had taken hold of Paul. Christ had ridden in on his stallion, catching Paul up in his arms with a love that would not let Paul go. But Paul did not want to flail loosely in Jesus' arms on this ride. He wanted to take hold of the One who had taken hold of him. *He wanted to know Christ.* In chapter two I noted how much better the ride with God is when we turn toward Jesus in his embrace and embrace him in return. In Job 42, Job turned in God's arms to embrace God as he held Job.

As he did with the apostle Paul, God had hold of Job all along, but Job had been flailing in God's arms, unable to come to terms with this new hard path God allowed in his life. I had been flailing in God's arms in my own path as well. I had thrown things, crying out angrily with one friend in particular with the news of the second tumor. I had questioned my pastors. And I had morosely walked the loop around my farmhouse, crying in God's presence, though I couldn't bring myself to envision his face or his goodness. Like an angry kid summoned to his parent's presence but refusing to look them in the eye, I had been stiff-necked with God, not out-wardly rebellious, but inwardly seething with anger and frustration. I didn't want to know Christ better. I wanted God to just leave me alone.

In Job 42, after much wrestling, Job submitted to God, turning in God's arms toward him, taking hold of the Redeemer as God had taken hold of Job. Job invited me to do so too. I too must bow my head in submission to God. I too must trust that he knows more than I, that his ways are better than mine. I grew in my fear of God and knowledge of the Holy One, but it was the kind of fear and knowledge that drew me toward him, not the kind that made me run away. God rode with me in his arms on a path I could not escape, and I needed to turn in his embrace and embrace him in return.

RESTORATION

After Job confessed his ignorance and submitted to God, the book of Job quickly concludes. Every sentence in those concluding verses packs a punch. God rebuked Job's friends, saying, "You have not spoken the truth about me, as my servant Job has." God told them to offer Job a burnt offering for themselves and have Job pray for them. He continued, "I will surely accept his prayer and not deal with you as your folly deserves" (Job 42:7-8). Even as Job hoped in the coming Redeemer, he became a picture of that Redeemer to his friends, an advocate before God for them. In this amazing moment, we see again that despite the back and forth of questions and correction between God and Job, Job remained in close relationship with God throughout his long ordeal. Job may have felt estranged from God at times, but God had taken hold of Job long before his trial, and he did not let go of Job during it.

Then God restored Job's fortunes.

When the CT scan showed the new tumor, it set off a convoluted series of events in my life. First, my new oncologist wanted to test my breast tumor for genetic markers because new research showed little benefit from chemotherapy for certain kinds of breast tumors. But she couldn't get the results from the old hospital in a timely manner. Results that were supposed to take days instead took weeks as we entered the Thanksgiving holidays. The wait between doctors' appointments or for test results or for rescheduled surgery after being postponed at the last minute has been a particularly vexing aspect of my medical path again and again.

The long-awaited results on my original cancerous tumor showed that there was a statistically negligible benefit to chemotherapy for my particular type of cancer. This convoluted path and scary new tumor had saved me from six months of debilitating chemotherapy! Doctors then quickly scheduled surgery to remove my abdominal tumor. I had that surgery the week before Christmas.

It took weeks to get the final biopsy results from that tumor. But in the new year I got the results that it too was not cancerous, though I showed signs of endometriosis. When I followed up with that doctor, he found precancerous cells in my uterus. And yet another invasive abdominal surgery was scheduled.

After yet more weeks of doctor's appointments and waiting for multiple surgery dates, I had that surgery. No new cancer was found. My colonoscopy came back clear, as did all of my genetic testing. As far as we know, I am cancer free. I can now see God's kindness to me in allowing each of these things to be discovered before any became life-threatening.

But as any sufferer knows, no amount of new blessings completely undoes the wounds left from the old. According to Job 42:11, Job's family and friends came by and continued to sympathize with him and offer comfort even after his fortunes were restored. Even though God gave Job more children, the loss of his first family was a wound he would never get over in this life. God has given me a newly remodeled home on the farm, a lovely respite as I have recovered from surgery after surgery. But I still feel the loss of home and life in Seattle, of the friends our family shared weekly playdates and watched every Super Bowl together, the church that walked closely with me through my divorce, and the families I spent Thanksgivings with when I was too far from my own family to make it home. Most of all, I feel deeply the loss of my husband. Like Job, when our suffering involves the loss of a family member or loved one, we may feel resolution and restoration in some areas, but we will always have a painful scar in others. I have scars on my body. I have more painful scars in my soul.

Despite the ongoing holes in his life and scars from his losses, Job lived a full and good life. He lived to see more children born and their children grown. He died full of days. For many of us though, there hasn't been such a turn in our fortunes toward good. We gain perspective from Job. He is our companion as he suffers. And he is our companion as he submits to God in it. But he is not our companion in his turn around of wealth, health, and family life.

I no longer have cancer, but the treatment to get rid of it has had ongoing ramifications. I already had type 1 diabetes and a type of juvenile arthritis that affected my life daily. I was able to manage both and function, but the surgeries and medicines to keep cancer at bay in my body have complicated both of those preexisting conditions. As I recovered from my last surgery, I finally realized over time that recovery wouldn't mean what I had hoped it would mean. Chronic illnesses eventually catch up with us, and mine have caught up with me.

And as I edit this book and read of the surgery scheduled a week before Christmas last year, I am prepping for yet another surgery scheduled—you guessed it—one week before Christmas this year.

I recently sat in an ER waiting room in acute pain from a complication from what I had hoped was my last surgery, I wrestled with the fact that, both physically and relationally, I haven't experienced the restoration Job had. I thought I had healed and my time regularly visiting hospitals was coming to a close. It demoralized me deeply to return to the ER in such pain weeks past the point I was supposed to be healed from surgery. The Spirit seemed to whisper in my ear, "Manna." When I felt demoralized because I was in crisis yet again, I needed manna for that day, even that hour. I needed the Bread of Life, equipping me not year by year, but hour by hour. "One day at a time, sweet Jesus" is no longer a cheesy song script but the utter need of my heart to survive. Like the children of Israel stuck in the wilderness, I remain dependent on daily manna from God until I see Jesus face to face.

TRUE COMFORT

Sufferers may turn to many different sources for comfort in their ongoing suffering. Some sources are helpful. Many more only mask the pain at hand. I have had to work hard to not give in to the temptation to numb the pain at my ongoing losses with alcohol, food, mindless amusement, or other unhealthy coping mechanisms. I've had to avoid ones that attempt to comfort me with lesser truths than the character of our sovereign God, which I have learned from Job. I have found only one true comfort, one true thing that moves me from flailing in my circumstances to rest and hope in them. It's believing that God exists in the middle of these circumstances and that he rewards those who diligently seek him. It's submitting to these rewards as he defines them, not as I or prosperity evangelists define them. It's looking day by day for the manna he provides and accepting it as it comes. And it's fearing God as the sovereign Creator of the universe who holds it all together. In that submission and reverential fear, I find the portion, the inheritance, that the psalmist of Psalm 73 found too. God holds me by my right hand, and afterward he will receive me to glory. As he did Job.

In the end God did not comfort Job with the words we might think he would use. Instead, God spoke counterintuitive words of comfort to Job. God is God, and you and I are not. Instead of chafing at this truth, Job submitted to God. And he guides us, as he sits with us in our tent of suffering, to do the same. In the moments of agitation as we wrestle with questions that cannot be answered, there is rest to be had in submitting to the Creator God as Job did. This is not a simple submission that doesn't allow for our cries of distress. Job teaches anything but that. But through our faith in the midst of our distress, the character of God is affirmed, and a great blow is given to Satan in the heavenly realm. Our testimony in these times may not be obvious to anyone else on earth, but it is obvious to Satan. And we have then, by Christ's help, won the war. "My righteous one will live by faith" (Hebrews 10:38).

REFLECT

Throughout Job's complaints to God in the book of Job, his friends "defend" God by saying in general that Job's suffering must be a consequence of his sin. In Job 42:7, God says, "I am angry with you and your two friends, for you have not spoken the truth about me, as my servant Job has." Job 8 is a good example. What subtle but faulty view of God did Bildad portray?

What images inspire you with the majesty and power of God?

Describe your perspective of their grandeur. (If you have the physical ability, it may bless you to spend time staring at the stars, the ocean, or a mountain range. If you can't physically get to such a majestic setting, I suggest the BBC Planet Earth or Blue Planet series.)

How does God's majesty in holding creation together inform how you think about your own path of life?

9

WAITING ON JESUS

Fellowship with Mary and Martha

The circumstances that led to my divorce are not ones I am free to detail in this book. Suffice it to say that I could see the train that threatened to destroy my family coming slowly but steadily down the tracks, our family stuck in a car in its path. But my desperate efforts to get us out of the car and off the tracks were ineffective, sometimes even seeming to speed up the train heading toward us rather than helping us escape it. I prayed desperately for God to supernaturally intervene because my efforts seemed to make things worse, not better. But the train kept coming, demolishing our family unit and everything we knew up to that point together as a family of four.

In my mind God could have intervened earlier than he did. He could have picked up the train and removed it from our path. He could have picked up our car and removed us from the train's path. But I waited, and no rescue came. My divorce was final, and my life left broken in pieces around me.

I am not the first person to look desperately for God's intervention and be left numbed in the aftermath of the devastation from his decision to wait. During that season, I was working on a book on God's interactions with women in the Gospels. I found much to ponder in Jesus' interaction with Mary and Martha about their brother's death, recorded in John 11. Their story echoed aspects of mine, and their emotions reflected the emotions I felt.

FRIENDS OF JESUS

Mary and Martha show up in Jesus' life more times with more detail than the majority of Jesus' male disciples. Simply put, they were his friends.

In an earlier scene in Luke 10:38-42, Jesus entered their village and was welcomed into their home. Martha seemed to be the older sister bearing greater responsibility and authority in the home. She was the one who welcomed Jesus into her home. She was also the one distracted from him by the many tasks of hospitality that fell on her shoulders while her sister sat at Jesus' feet listening to his teaching. Luke says in verse 40 that "Martha was distracted by her many tasks, and she came up and asked, 'Lord, don't you care that my sister has left me to serve alone? So tell her to give me a hand.'" Jesus answered her, "Martha, Martha, you are worried and upset about many things, but one thing is necessary. Mary has made the right choice, and it will not be taken away from her."

Was this the first time Jesus was in Martha's home? We don't know for sure. It is the first record of such in the Gospels, but Martha's boldness to ask Jesus for help from her sister suggests a familiarity with him from previous interactions.

Jesus rebukes Martha, but the passage doesn't suggest he responded harshly. "Martha," he says, "you are worried and upset about many things." Before her brother ever contracted the illness that caused his death, Martha was worried and upset about other things. The Greek word for *upset* indicates turbulence.[1] As an apple cart is upset when a wheel falls off, apples tumbling out and falling ruined on the hard ground, Martha's well-planned day had been too. Before my most intense season of suffering set in, my day too was often upset by unexpected crises, big and small. A child is sick, and this derails my carefully planned schedule for the day. Years later, I am diagnosed with cancer, and it creates turbulence in my planned schedule for the next decade. Circumstances, large and small, come along in our lives on a regular basis that upset our apple cart. My cart often seems full of more responsibilities than the cart can hold, and I try diligently to keep them from spilling over the sides. The result is internal turbulence. I am unsteady, unable to cope, with apples continually falling to the ground among the responsibilities I juggle.

Jesus was not concerned about food or whatever other aspects of hosting a crowd that were causing Martha's turbulence that day. After all, this is the man who had just fed a large multitude with only five loaves and two fishes. Surely Martha was aware of that miracle. Perhaps she had even been a part of the crowd that he fed. But I cannot cast stones at Martha, for I am regularly distracted from the eternally important thing in a setting by other trappings that make it temporarily physically comfortable. I, like Martha, often experience turbulence in my well-planned days.

"One thing is necessary," Jesus said to Martha in his reply. One thing preceded all the others in value, and that thing had preeminence because it was a necessity while the others things were not. In Mary and Martha's case, sitting at Jesus' feet and listening to his teaching was a necessity. The distractions of hospitality were not. Hospitality can be helpful. It makes folks comfortable. But apparently no one was starving to death, and Jesus deemed it a lesser priority. When we must choose between that which makes us comfortable and that which is necessary for life, Jesus taught Martha to choose the necessity.

Jesus called what Mary was doing, learning at his feet, the "right choice." The Greek word for choice means a share, portion, or distinct part of the whole.[2] The King James Version says "that good part." Among all the opportunities for the day that Jesus' presence in their house offered them, Mary had chosen the good portion. In sitting at Jesus' feet, she had chosen the best morsel, the prime cut of the offerings extended to her family that day. Like Asaph in Psalm 73, she points us to God himself as the thing that satisfies us.

Every day I am faced with a similar smorgasbord of choices as Mary and Martha were, but my plate can only hold so much. My kids, my cat, my dog, my morning cup of coffee, and the responsibilities of my home and job all grab at the portions of my day. Of all the good and right responsibilities I have in a given day, one is utterly necessary. One offers the Living Water to my soul; one sustains me for the others in a way nothing else can. Only one portion offers the peace that keeps the other responsibilities from upsetting me in a way that I am actually useless, at least temporarily, to the very ones competing for my resources. The irony in Luke 10 is that Martha had gotten so worked up by the demands of hospitality that she actually was not being hospitable, interrupting Jesus' time teaching in her home.

This teaching moment between Mary, Martha, and Jesus sets the stage for the next one in John 11. Mary and Martha needed the necessary portion that came from Jesus' teaching, the doctrine and theology that he taught his followers, for the days ahead. They remind me that I need it too. They were about to lose their brother, and in the coming persecution of the church after Jesus' resurrection, they likely lost much more. Though there was a great crowd following Jesus at this point, soon the crowd would change from calling out "Hosanna" to shouting "Crucify him." During the siege of Jerusalem forty years after Jesus' death, many more would lose family, homes, and even the temple that had been the center of their religious experience for generations. Would Mary and Martha still be alive at the time of the dispersion? Were they forced to flee their home and the land of their birth as their Jewish neighbors were? The sustaining truths they learned at Jesus' feet would be theirs forever, unshaken by future trials. Roman invaders could not rob them of the truths they learned at Jesus' feet. This teaching was necessary sustenance for the days ahead. Mary whispers to us in our tent of suffering, in the midst of the chaos and many balls to juggle that come with our long trials, not to forget to sit at Jesus' feet and learn from him through the Scriptures. Of all the things that require our attention, learning from him through the Scriptures is the most necessary part, the sustaining provision that sees us through the rest.

LAZARUS'S DEATH

Luke 10 gives us context for understanding the emotions between Mary and Martha and their teacher and friend Jesus, as they wait on Jesus to come to heal Lazarus in John 11. Mary and Martha sent a message to Jesus, "Lord, the one you love is sick." Jesus' response is important: "When Jesus heard it, he said, 'This sickness will not end in death but is for the glory of God, so that the Son of God may be glorified through it.' Now Jesus loved Martha, her sister, and Lazarus. So when he heard that he was sick, he stayed two more days in the place where he was" (John 11:4-6).

If you miss verses 5 and 6, you miss the entire point of this story. Jesus deliberately waited until Lazarus had died, and then he answered Mary and Martha's request that he come to them. Because he loved them.

When Martha heard Jesus was finally coming, she went to meet him. But Mary remained seated in the house. Martha confronts Jesus, "If you had been here, my brother wouldn't have died." Jesus assures her that her brother will rise again. Then Martha summons Mary, and Mary falls at Jesus' feet in distress with a similar cry, "Lord, if you had been here, my brother would not have died!"

> When Jesus saw her crying, and the Jews who had come with
> her crying, he was deeply moved in his spirit and troubled.
> "Where have you put him?" he asked.
>
> "Lord," they told him, "come and see."
> Jesus wept. (John 11:32-35)

WAITING ON JESUS

Again and again I am struck that Jesus deliberately waited to answer Mary and Martha's summons until after Lazarus died. His purpose in this delay seems twofold, but not distinctly twofold like a mutually exclusive Venn diagram. His two purposes overlap greatly, and both were served by Jesus' intentional delay until after Lazarus died.

What were Jesus' purposes in this delay? First, Jesus said Lazarus's sickness would end with Jesus being glorified as God. Second, John's account says that Jesus loved this little family. John then used an important connecting word in verse 6, "*So* when he heard that he was sick, he stayed two more days in the place where he was" (John 11:6, emphasis mine). At first, this deliberate delay in going to the sisters seemed cruel to me. If it did not seem deliberately cruel to Mary and Martha, it at least felt confusing. They did not understand why Jesus waited to come. The sisters believed in Jesus and were committed to him. They rightly carried their message of need to him in faith when Lazarus was deathly ill. Yet Jesus waited two more days before turning toward them when he could have returned and healed Lazarus immediately.

John tells us that what at first appears cruel was actually motivated by Jesus' love for this family. He was not hardened toward them. He had an intimate familial relationship with them. He loved them, sacrificially caring about them, valuing their good above his own. So he waited two more days to come.

With the hindsight we have as believers who grew up hearing the story of Lazarus's resurrection, we understand how Jesus' love for them was consistent with his next actions. But his love isn't demonstrated simply because he raised Lazarus from the dead. He could have similarly shown his love for them by healing Lazarus from his illness and saving Mary and Martha the agony of Lazarus's death. Jesus loved them with something greater still, by showing through their little family that he was God with authority over death. He loved them by revealing to them his glory. They wanted him to heal Lazarus. He wanted to show them he was God.

In verse 15, after Lazarus died, Jesus told his disciples, "I'm glad for you that I wasn't there so that you may believe." He loved his disciples, and he loved Lazarus's family. Because he loved them, He wanted them to see face-to-face his power as God and his authority over death. None of his authority as God to defeat even death could have been shown if Jesus had not waited to come to them.

As Mary and Martha sit with me in my own tent of suffering, I can imagine how it felt to them in the hours leading to Lazarus' death, hearing nothing from their beloved friend, and the days after when Jesus still seemed to be avoiding them. Though we know the resolution to God's temporary silence to Mary, Martha, and Lazarus, many of us experience our own similar silence now, and we do not yet know how God will work it out for us. I imagine for most reading this, God's silence in our suffering has lasted longer than a few days. We do not yet understand how things will resolve in a way that is consistent with both God's love for us and his own glory. We have not yet seen the provision that gets us out of financial ruin, the reconciliation of our broken relationships, or the physical healing of our dying loved one. God hasn't yet caused our loved one who died to rise from the grave.

Depending on the length of our season of waiting, the period between calling out to God for help and seeing God move to answer, we may recognize ourselves in either Martha's or Mary's response to Jesus. Martha responded boldly, "Where were you, Lord? If you had been here, Lazarus wouldn't have died." Martha still verbalized a measure of belief. She knew that Jesus could have healed Lazarus and believed still that Jesus would heal him in the last day, and she easily gave vent to her frustration waiting for him.

Mary's response was different. In terms of the ancient theory of personality types popularized by Hippocrates, Mary seemed melancholic.[3] The Gospels portray her as quiet and thoughtful. Though outward displays of emotion like Martha's get folks labeled as emotional or high-spirited, the emotions of quiet, reserved people often run much deeper and are more painful than others recognize. Mary knew as Martha did that Jesus approached. But while Martha quickly ran to Jesus giving vent verbally to her frustration at his tarrying, Mary held back. I envision her sitting quietly, staring at a drawing on the wall of her room, numb from both the shock of her brother's death and the despair edging at her subconscious that the one she so loved and worshiped had not come to help. She had looked to the right place for rescue, but the rescue did not come. I imagine she felt pain too difficult to contemplate at that moment.

Yet, when she got word that Jesus was calling for her specifically, she was pulled from her quiet, turbulent thoughts, and she too went quickly to Jesus. When she saw him, the emotions that she had successfully stamped down came spilling out in an avalanche. She fell at Jesus' feet weeping, "Lord, if You had been here, my brother wouldn't have died" (John 11:32). Martha felt frustrated. Mary felt betrayed.

Jesus saw her weeping. He saw Lazarus's neighbors and friends weeping. He stood among the turbulence of the fallen world around him, and it affected him. Verse 33 says he became troubled and deeply moved by all that distressed his friends. The fall ushered in turbulent despair in the world at large and in our smaller individual families. The King of kings felt this turbulence with this little family and did a profound thing. He wept too. He doesn't stand far off from us, "unable to sympathize with our weaknesses" (Hebrews 4:15). He saw Mary's grief and was affected by it. He felt with Lazarus's family and friends all that was wrong with this world, symbolized in this little moment.

We know how this story ends; most of us learned it in Sunday school. Jesus then raised Lazarus from the dead, stunning the crowd. Jesus had been miraculously defying the laws of nature for some time now. But with this miracle he showed his glory as God and his authority over even death. Most believers take that truth for granted now, believing with Martha that, in the end, he will raise our loved ones and make all things right. But until I reach that day when all things are made right, I am more comforted by the fact that Jesus felt the turbulence with Mary and Martha, and with me, in the waiting.

Jesus understood Mary's feelings and sympathized with her despair. Why? Because he entered her suffering. He enters ours too. He doesn't watch our suffering from the outside. He walks into it with us, bearing it with us. But so too he calls us to enter his as well (1 Peter 4:13; Philippians 3:10). And this is the crux of real relationship, the mutuality of shared burden, even the burden of grief. As Jesus entered Mary's turbulent grief, the next scenes of John have her entering his, anointing Jesus' feet for burial, recognizing that he would die as the Lamb of God well before the rest of his disciples understood this truth.

In the Garden of Eden humans were not created in perfection to weep at the death of a loved one. We were not created in perfection to break faith with our spouses or to bury our children. We were not created with fears or grief. These elements entered the world at the fall.

The griefs and frustrations that agitate us today agitated Jesus as well, to the point that he willingly laid down his life to defeat sin and death once and for all. As we wait on his kingdom to be fully realized and all that was lost in the fall to be restored, I am comforted that Jesus walks with me in the waiting, feeling the unrest and turbulence I feel, with love for me and a vision for his own glory.

Andrew Wilson, writing of his family's struggles with two special-needs children and his subsequent wrestling with God, makes this poignant observation:

We worship a crying God—a God who became like us, suffered bereavement and loss, wept at gravesides, and cried out in anguish as he died. So when we experience suffering and face all the unanswered *whys?*, we may never know what the answer is, but we know for sure what the answer *isn't*. It isn't because God doesn't love us. It isn't because God doesn't care. It isn't because he is distant or unsympathetic or cold or merciless.[4]

Despite knowing he would soon raise Lazarus from the dead, Jesus wept when faced with the grief Mary and Martha experienced as they waited on him to come to them. His tears reflected that old name from Isaiah, the Man of Sorrows, acquainted with grief (Isaiah 53:3 KJV). Jesus was not undisturbed by their suffering. He experienced its turbulence with them. He is able to come alongside us in our suffering too, nourishing us in our journey as we wait on all things to be made new. In Mary and Martha's case, he stalled not to torment them more but because he loved them. The despair of the long waiting period only served as a spotlight on the glory of God revealed in the end. That glory is worth knowing. Jesus raised Lazarus from the dead, and shortly after, Jesus rose from the dead himself. One day we and our loved ones will all rise as well. May Mary and Martha's story comfort you today as you wait for your own resolution, your own resurrection.

REFLECT

Do you identify more with Mary or Martha in your response to frustration and suffering? In what ways?

John 11:5-6 says, "Jesus loved Martha, her sister, and Lazarus. So when he heard that [Lazarus] was sick, he stayed two more days in the place where he was." How do you feel when you read that Jesus received this request to come and waited instead until Lazarus died?

Have you experienced God waiting to intervene in your suffering until it seemed too late? If Job, Mary, and Martha were to sit across the table from you, what encouragement might they give you about God with respect to your own specific unresolved suffering?

FELLOWSHIP WITH THE CLOUD OF WITNESSES

In **These Strange Ashes** famed missionary Elisabeth Elliot recounts her first missionary journey to Ecuador, concluding with the loss of the suitcase holding all of her translation work and the deaths of the two translators who had helped her gather it.

> Maria and Macario were dead and buried. The mission station was demolished. Even the most sinewy faith in the world could not bring them back. But hope still survived for the suitcase. The Lord whose eyes run to and fro throughout the whole earth knew where that suitcase and its precious contents were. I prayed for its recovery. Surely, Lord . . . ?
>
> The suitcase did not turn up.
>
> And so it often is. Faith, prayer, and obedience are our requirements. We are not offered in exchange immunity and exemption from the world's woes. What we are offered has to do with another world altogether.[1]

My father-in-law sent me *These Strange Ashes* after my mother-in-law was diagnosed with cancer in her fifties and died shortly after.

He was a missionary pastor, and she had been his right-hand help in ministry, a trained elementary teacher who loved teaching Sunday school and playing the piano for their small church services. In *These Strange Ashes*, my father-in-law found camaraderie with Elisabeth Elliott as she recounted the lessons in the sovereignty of God on her first missionary journey, lessons she would need at multiple points in her life in the following years. The book ended with all of her work from that first missionary journey laying in ashes around her feet, though years later God rebuilt it through a different missionary family who came along behind her. The lessons in faith from her first missionary journey formed the scaffolding that held Elliot up through the next decades of her extraordinary life and ministry.

I first read *These Strange Ashes* as the ministry I had moved across the country for began to fall apart. I had been deacon of women's theology and training at a church planting megachurch, training women in the deep things of the Scriptures, the most fulfilling job I've ever had. In the middle of my own ministry in the church, other church leaders became embroiled in an angry internal fight for control. In a few short years this church that had ten thousand attendees during Sunday services ended up closing its doors and dissolving its legal status. It was a stunning, sobering turn of events in my life watching the ministry I had loved dismantled by angry conflict and sinful leadership practices.

I read *These Strange Ashes* again a few years later as I sat in the ashes of my own marriage. The title reflected how I felt about the ruins around me. They felt strange, unusual, and surprising. They unsettled me as I grappled to understand what had happened to my life and plans for the future. Like Elliot, I felt disassociated from those ashes for a while, pondering them from afar for the strange and unexpected things they were before I could enter the depths of grief associated with each.

Elliot submitted to God in her unanswered questions—just as Job did—and continued walking by faith, not by sight. The disaster of her first missionary journey gave me context for the faith that her future extraordinary missionary pursuits exhibited. As I sat in my own heap of confusing ashes of the life I had known, Elliot encouraged me to get up and continue walking forward too.

I found encouragement to persevere through another of Elliot's works as well, her biography of Amy Carmichael, *A Chance to Die*. Both Elliot and Carmichael persevered in faith through many grave setbacks in their work and close relationships. I have found similar encouragement through spirituals, the musical legacy of a people whose faith persevered through generations of injustice and oppression.

> My brother and my sister, you have trials like me
> When we are trying to serve the Lord
> And win the victory
> Old Satan fight us hard
> Our journey to retard
> But a little talk with Jesus make it right.[2]

I sing to myself, "When the saints come marching in, I want to be one of them," and I think of those who have gone on before me, in much worse persecution than I face today, singing together their perseverance in the faith aloud to one another.[3] It isn't only living friends or characters in Scripture who sit with us in our tent of suffering, offering encouragement along the way. Though now dead, Elliot, Carmichael, and a host of persevering Christians, many names lost as a direct result of their oppression, have all become part of the cloud of witnesses the author of Hebrews discusses in Hebrews 11–12, sharing with me the struggles of their own journey and cheering me and you on from the sidelines in ours.

NOT BY SIGHT

"We walk by faith, not by sight" (2 Corinthians 5:7). The apostle Paul reminded believers in Corinth that they walked by faith, not by seeing clearly what was at their feet or the next steps ahead. But sometimes we twist an ankle in that walk. As Paul exhorted Gentile believers in Corinth to walk by faith when they couldn't see ahead, the author of Hebrews wrote to Jewish believers to stir up hope and perseverance in a discouraged church, limping along with clearly twisted ankles in the faith. Apparently, some were wilting in their Christian walk, needing to be retaught truth they should have been ready to teach to others (Hebrews 5:12). Some weren't even attending their church gatherings anymore (Hebrews 10:25). They were languishing in the faith, and I found the encouragement in Hebrews to those limping believers a comforting companion as my faith languished, and I too limped along.

The author of Hebrews taught that, without faith, it is impossible to please God (Hebrews 11:6). Like Paul, he taught that a faith pleasing to God endures as proof of what is not seen (Hebrews 11:1). If we saw our circumstances all working out as we expected, we would not experience the furnace that forges the kind of faith we see in those who suffer for extended seasons. Like Job's long season of suffering without understanding God's purposes in it, *this very perseverance in seasons of silence without seeing God's solution is the essence of faith.* Simply put, faith exists because we cannot yet see what we hope for. We use the language of tested faith in relation to long seasons of suffering. Suffering tests faith. It proves that our faith is real because we walk by faith when we can no longer walk by sight.

The author of Hebrews instructs a limping church about to go through even more serious testing through the dispersion and destruction of the temple. The letter reminded believers of the cloud of witnesses in whom God had forged such faith before them. These long-dead brothers and sisters in Christ who encouraged the church in Hebrews encourage us today as well. Like cheering supporters on the sidelines of a marathon, they cheer us on to persevere today and offer cooling nourishment along the way.

ABEL, ENOCH, AND NOAH

By faith Abel offered to God a better sacrifice than Cain did. . . .

By faith Enoch was taken away, and so he did not experience death. . . .

By faith Noah, after he was warned about what was not yet seen and motivated by godly fear, built an ark to deliver his family. (Hebrews 11:4-5, 7)

Abel, Enoch, and Noah, much like Job, offer us glimpses of faith among those who knew only the most basic revelation of God to his children. During their days, the world already had a lot of problems, but God had not yet given much instruction in light of it. After the fall, God spoke the first gospel message in Genesis 3:15. He would send one, born of woman, who would give Satan a knockout blow to the head. Abel, Enoch, and Noah likely knew at least that much. How much more did they understand? We do not know.

The little nugget of truth from Genesis 3:15 that they likely did know is the essence of our faith today. That is the bud forming on the stalk that eventually unfurls in the New Testament into the good news of Jesus in all his glory. One was coming who would soundly defeat Satan. Our faith says that Jesus came and dealt Satan that deathblow, though we "do not yet see everything subjected to him" (Hebrews 2:8). The ultimate defeat of Satan and the banishment of all the pain and heartache the fall thrust upon the world remains essential to our faith today.

Abel, Enoch, and Noah did not see this bud unfurl or this flower form in their lifetime. They did not see this defeater of Satan come in person, but they looked from afar for him and walked in faith believing God would send him. And in that context, they obeyed.

ABRAHAM, SARAH, AND JACOB

> By faith Abraham, when he was called, obeyed and set out for a place that he was going to receive as an inheritance. He went out, even though he did not know where he was going. . . .
>
> By faith even Sarah herself, when she was unable to have children, received power to conceive offspring. . . .
>
> By faith Jacob, when he was dying, blessed each of the sons of Joseph. (Hebrews 11: 8, 11, 21)

This next set of witnesses who cheer us from the sidelines would do it with heads held low if God had not fully removed their condemnation through Christ's sacrifice on the cross. Their stories of faith had profound low points. Among other things, Sarah didn't believe that God would give her a son in her old age, and both she and Abraham abused Hagar in their lack of faith. Jacob, as well, was a liar and a swindler. But later in their lives, by God's grace and mercy, each ended their walk faithfully and instilled that faith in the next generation. The mere fact that their names are mentioned at all in this list of the faithful is a trophy not of their righteousness but of God's great mercy. Whether we don't understand what God is doing or have blatantly sinned in light of the truth we do know, others have persevered before us despite similar failure, and they encourage us that God's mercy, grace, and forgiveness will enable us to do the same.

Verse 13 says a beautiful thing about these folks whose faith was pocked with moments of weakness and stumbling. "These all died in faith, although they had not received the things that were promised. But they saw them from a distance, greeted them, and confessed that they were foreigners and temporary residents on the earth."

They saw their promised destination from afar and died before they reached it on earth. Their faith was not sight. But they lived believing that those promises would be fulfilled. And they were.

JOSEPH

No one better demonstrated embracing from a distance something they wouldn't fully experience in their earthly lifetime than Joseph, of whom Hebrews 11:22 says, "By faith Joseph, as he was nearing the end of his life, mentioned the exodus of the Israelites and gave instructions concerning his bones."

Joseph's story is given in Genesis 37–50. Sunday school lessons about him that I heard in childhood focused on Joseph's faithfulness until his earthly reconciliation with his brothers who had sold him into slavery. His struggles made sense once his brothers came to him in need of the food that Joseph foresaw to put away, food that saved their family from extinction. Yet, when the author of Hebrews references Joseph in Hebrews 11, he is commended for something altogether different. By instructing his sons to take his bones with them to the Promised Land, he revealed his conviction that God was doing something that transcended Joseph's life on earth just as he had promised to Joseph's great-grandfather Abraham. The fact that the ultimate resolution to his suffering on earth wouldn't be realized until long after his death did not deter Joseph from his confidence that it would truly happen. That is the essence of faith that is not sight.

In the middle of his affliction, before any reconciliation with his brothers, Joseph fathered two sons. "And the second son he named Ephraim and said, 'God has made me fruitful in the land of my affliction'" (Genesis 41:52). *Fruitful in the land of my affliction.* Many thoughts hit me as I meditate on why Joseph named his son Ephraim (which sounds like the Hebrew word for *fruitful*). With this name, Joseph hands me a cup of cold water to first sip from and then pour over my head in my weariness in my own marathon. Though his bones would not stay in that land forever, Joseph died in the land of his affliction. But he was fruitful in that land of exile for the time he was there.

Like God's words to Job when he finally spoke from the whirlwind, this name for Joseph's son is counterintuitive. It does not reflect what most of us expect the result of the sins against Joseph to be. Joseph was fruitful in the very place that should have sucked the life out of him. That paradox intrigues me. To be honest, I initially resisted identifying with the name Ephraim because for a long time I dug my heels in the ground and refused to consider being fruitful in the land of my affliction. I wanted God to end my affliction, and then I wanted to be fruitful in the beautiful land I imagined would be God's best for his children. But it eventually became clear that I was powerless to end the troubles, physically and relationally, that plagued me. The result was looking to God to move on my behalf and subsequent impatience with him when he didn't.

In contrast, Joseph was fruitful in the waiting. And he cheers me on with the hope that I can be too. When I objectively step back from my emotions in my own suffering, I see that no one in Scripture seems to be fruitful *except* in the land of their affliction. In fact, you can argue from Scripture that suffering, affliction, and death to self are essential to God's plan for fruitfulness in his children. "Truly I tell you, unless a grain of wheat falls to the ground and dies, it remains by itself. But if it dies, it produces much fruit" (John 12:24).

In the midst of waiting for my affliction to end and God's kingdom to come in my life and home, meditating on Joseph's example and encouragement from the sidelines has blessed me greatly. What does it look like to be fruitful in the very places I most long to be delivered from? Joseph's story reminds me that my suffering doesn't end the possibility of fruitfulness but instead may be the very thing that prepares the ground for fruit that remains. "You did not choose Me but I chose you, and appointed you that you would go and bear fruit, and that your fruit would remain" (John 15:16 NASB).

A VARIETY OF WITNESSES

Hebrews 11 continues naming witnesses that encourage us from the sidelines—Moses, Rahab, Gideon, Barak, Samson, Jephthah, David, Samuel, and the prophets. I am surprised by several who are mentioned, yet their inclusion in this list, often despite great failures, encourages me. Hebrews 11:39-40 says that "all these were approved through their faith, but they did not receive what was promised, since God had provided something better for us, so that they would not be made perfect without us."

At this point the variety of brothers and sisters cheering us on from the sidelines is clear. As I pointed out in chapter three on fellowship in the body of Christ, each of them has a distinct story of suffering, just as each of us does. My story of cancer is different from yours. Other's circumstances around broken families are different from mine. Even in the death of a spouse, parent, or child, the circumstances of that death and paths of grief that flow from it are widely varied. The maturity from God's comfort in our suffering enables us to draw encouragement to persevere from one another, not a one-to-one correlation between our suffering and another's.

The thing that unifies those in Hebrew's list of the faithful is what they all are, not what they all experienced. They are all witnesses. "Therefore, since we also have such a large cloud of witnesses surrounding us, let us lay aside every hindrance and the sin that so easily ensnares us. Let us run with endurance the race that lies before us" (Hebrews 12:1).

I love courtroom documentaries on TV. After each of my surgeries I watched countless episodes of *Forensic Files*, *Dateline*, and *48 Hours* as I sat on my sofa recovering. I was particularly vexed by the story of Russ Faria, convicted of murdering his wife despite four alibi witnesses who put him miles away playing games with them at the time of her murder.[4] He spent four years in prison before a judge overturned his conviction. Another woman later convicted of a separate murder is now the prime suspect in the murder of Russ's wife. Turns out, the four witnesses corroborating his alibi on the witness stand were all telling the truth. Police, prosecutors, and jury discounted the most important evidence in the trial, the verbal testimony of multiple eyewitnesses testifying to the same truth—Russ was with them. By ignoring this eyewitness testimony, prosecutors and police left the real murderer free to strike again.

By definition, a witness is one who gives evidence. The witness testifies of what they have seen, and that testimony becomes part of the body of evidence that indicates whether something is true or not.[5] When multiple witnesses testifying to the same evidentiary fact are ignored or discounted by prosecutors or a jury, it leads to grave miscarriages of justice. From the grave, Elisabeth Elliot and Amy Carmichael testify of God's faithfulness and trustworthiness to me. Through their writings, they enter my tent and bear witness, and their witness becomes part of the body of evidence that indicates God truly is trustworthy. I would be a fool to ignore the testimony they present.

What did Abraham, Joseph, Rahab, and Elisabeth Elliot all witness? What do their words still testify to? They do not give evidence of their own faith but of God's faithfulness to them. They are runners who ran the race before us, whose path was as difficult if not more than ours, whose legs felt as tired as ours. They are runners who stumbled, who doubted, and who sometimes gravely sinned. They don't shout from the sidelines, "You can do it!" They shout, "God's not giving up on you. He'll carry you across the finish line himself." They testify that God will hold us tightly through grave injustice. We will make it to the end just as they made it to the end because we all believe in the same God, who remains faithful to us, holding us up even when we stumble. Stumbling, limping marathoners, suffering in the later miles of a frustratingly long journey, don't despair. God will not let you fall. He will carry you across the finish line. "Let us hold on to the confession of our hope without wavering, since he who promised is faithful" (Hebrews 10:23).

SOURCE AND PROTECTOR OF FAITH

Hebrews 12:2 goes on to tell us to keep "our eyes on Jesus, the source and perfecter of our faith." The Greek word translated "source" is *archēgos*, a combination of *archē*, the beginning or origin of something, and *agō*, to lead.[6] Like a king leading his army into battle, Jesus is the leader at the front line of our battle for faith when we cannot see. Jesus is also the protector or perfecter of that faith. He is both the source of the equipment that we use to win the battle—the king providing horses, ammunition, and shields to those who follow behind him—and the one who runs to our defense when we are knocked down. He leads us into battle, he is the source of our resources in that battle, and he protects us throughout the battle.

This chapter didn't begin with our fellowship with Jesus, but this book did. The cloud of human witnesses this chapter focuses on are not the point of this faith. They instead are witnesses who point us to the beginning and end point of our faith, Jesus Christ.

Hebrews 11:39-40 says, "They did not receive what was promised, since God had provided something better for us, so that they would not be made perfect without us." These Old Testament believers in Hebrews 11–12 were walking in faith hoping for something better, something that wouldn't be completed until Christ came hundreds of years later and reconciled all the elect unto himself. Their story isn't completed until ours is, when we all stand with Jesus at the marriage supper of the Lamb, gloriously reconciled to God and each other. None of these long-dead witnesses will be made perfect without us. No believer gets left behind, and so they cheer each of us on, testifying to God's faithfulness to get us over the finish line as he did them. Jesus loses none of his own.

We have come full circle, as these companions in our journey give testimony in the courtroom of the truth of the person and work of Jesus Christ and the faithfulness of God to fulfill his promises. They give evidence that holds us fast when we cannot see for ourselves. I too give evidence now of God's faithfulness to me when I could not see, when my eyes perceived only darkness and dense fog ahead of me, obscuring any purpose to my suffering or hope for peace or joy as I walked the road laid before me. You will give such evidence to those who come behind you in this marathon as well.

REFLECT

Hebrews 11 was written to persecuted Jewish believers about to endure even more hardship through the destruction of the temple and the dispersion of the Jews. It gives examples of persecuted believers who have gone before us who witness to us today of God's faithfulness to the bitter end. Do any among those listed in the chapter mirror aspects of your struggles? Who?

How would their testimony help persecuted and discouraged Hebrew believers?

How does their testimony help you today?

Rahab's story is given in Joshua 2 and 6. In Joshua 2:8-13, she speaks about God. What would she testify to you today about God if she were able to talk to you?

Has any Christian witness (not from Scripture) testified to you from the grave of God's faithfulness? Who? What about their story has most encouraged you?

FELLOWSHIP WITH
THE ROCK

There's a scene in *Star Wars:* *The Last Jedi* in which Finn, the former stormtrooper turned rebel fighter, falls in a deep hole in the crumbling cargo bay of the emperor's ship during his fight with his nemesis, Captain Phasma. As his cohort Rose gasps in horror at Finn's sure demise, Phasma turns to fire on her. But behind her in the background, Finn rises from the gaping hole on some kind of hydraulic lift that caught him when he fell. He goes on to defeat Phasma and help save the day. I love that scene. We all need such a lift to catch us when we fall and raise us back up to action.

I had been clawing to get back on sure footing in my marriage for a season, but after getting a foothold and seeming to move toward a surer foundation, new circumstances blew me into the abyss, with nothing to grab as I fell. In the two years after my divorce, I seemed to find some footing again, but the discovery of breast cancer that had spread to a lymph node sent me into free fall all over again. In a span of a few short years, life as I knew it had been destroyed not once but twice.

If you have suffered for any length of time, you know the moment you too felt your feet slip off your secure earthly foundation, backed into an abyss by your spiritual nemesis, Satan. You may have lost your health, your bank account, or an important relationship. Perhaps you lost someone so close to you that it feels like you lost a piece of yourself. Suffering involves the loss of something or someone we were counting on. We were walking along with our feet on firm ground, or so we thought, but suddenly the ground crumbled under us, and we were in free fall. How can you stand firm against the schemes of the devil (Ephesians 6:10) when you can't find footing at all?

We cannot function without a firm foundation. We need planted feet. When the foundation we have built our lives on falls apart, believers have another surer foundation under us that stops our free fall and raises us back up when we are powerless to do so ourselves. Jesus is our companion in suffering. But even more than that, he is our sure foundation in suffering that catches us when the abyss seems to swallow us.

THE ROCK OF ISRAEL

In Genesis 49 Jacob is the first to call God a rock in Scripture. As he speaks words of blessing over his sons before his death, Jacob stops over Joseph and says,

> Joseph is a fruitful vine,
> a fruitful vine beside a spring;
> its branches climb over the wall.
> The archers attacked him,
> shot at him, and were hostile toward him.
> Yet his bow remained steady,

and his strong arms were made agile
by the hands of the Mighty One of Jacob,
by the name of the Shepherd, the Rock of Israel.
  (Genesis 49:22-24)

Joseph's decades of suffering began with his brothers literally throwing him in a pit. When he lost his footing, pushed into a pit so deep he couldn't scale its walls on his own, he lost control of his life and his future. The depth of those walls kept him from his father and younger brother. They kept him from freedom. Even when he was dragged out of the physical walls of the pit, he was engulfed in the deeper walls of slavery in a foreign country, including the walls of a dungeon for a season. Yet Jacob speaks of the profound fruitfulness that Joseph, who named his son "fruitful in the land of my affliction," experienced not in spite of but directly through circumstances that should have crushed him.

Why did Joseph's pit of captivity and oppression not engulf and destroy him? How did Joseph find footing in such terrible circumstances? By the hands of the Mighty One of Jacob and by the name of the Shepherd, the Rock of Israel. The almighty Rock of Israel caught Joseph when he lost control of his life and lifted him up to positions of power and authority over the very ones who sold him into slavery. The almighty Rock of Israel blessed Joseph with Egypt's bounty, but more importantly, he blessed Joseph with a heavenly bounty (Genesis 49:25).

The first mention of a word or concept in Scripture is always important. This first mention of God as Rock in Scripture is in the context of one forced into great suffering not of his own doing. Joseph was attacked, surrounded by hostile oppressors. But by the hands of God, Joseph's bow remained steady and his arms agile for battle. No cramp set in his arms as he waited for God to work on his behalf. The Rock was under him, holding him up, and the result was a man who, at the end of his painful journey, had been fruitful in a land of hostile oppression and affliction. He was a fruitful vine whose branches scaled the walls of his confinement, blessed by God and a blessing to many others, in the very place that should have sucked the life out of him.

ROCK OF REFUGE

God is called a Stone, Rock, or Cornerstone with regularity through the rest of Scripture. In Deuteronomy 32:4, Moses used this name to emphasize the steadfast attributes of God that we can count on in a crisis.

> The Rock—his work is perfect;
> all his ways are just.
> A faithful God, without bias,
> he is righteous and true.

God's work is perfect. His ways are just. He's faithful, without bias or injustice. He is righteous and upright. His words are true, and we can count on what he says. These are the things about God that make him the sure foundation beneath us when everything else gives way. These are the things that Moses testifies to us as a firsthand witness of God's steadfast faithfulness.

David found God his rock as well.

> The LORD is my rock,
> my fortress, and my deliverer,
> my God, my rock where I seek refuge,
> my shield and the horn of my salvation,
> my stronghold. (Psalm 18:2)

David here presents God our Rock as the place he could safely hide. God was the fortress in which David could retreat and find refuge. Like Asaph in Psalm 73, David hid in the sanctuary of God in times of distress. The Rock of Israel was Joseph's Shepherd and David's hiding place. He was the shield that defended David from attack.

If I ever get caught up in a national emergency, I hope I'm in or near a Costco. If the power goes out, they've got flashlights and batteries. They've got generators and their own gas station to fuel them. They've got food and drinks to spare, clothes if we are cold, and fans if we are hot. They even have medicine and beds.

Both Jacob's words and David's words in Psalm 18 present God as a one-stop shop for rescue. God is the Costco of rescue and refuge. In the single source of God, we find a variety of help. We find a safe place to rest and get the nourishment we need to recoup. God is the fortress who protects us from the storms outside, and he is the refuge that allows us to find new supplies, safe from destruction though the winds still rage around us. He gives us shields and weapons and a horn to use to call for greater supplies, those supplied through our union with Christ.

David's language in Psalm 18 reminds me of Paul's in Ephesians 6. There, Paul exhorts us to put on the helmet of salvation, the sword of the Spirit, and the shield of faith, which are available to us in this fortress (Ephesians 6:16-17). We get the gospel of peace as the new shoes to protect our feet and give us the cushion we need to finish our marathon along our rocky path (v. 15). The equipment and nourishment we need to endure are available to us in one store only, the refuge of God himself. But in that one store all things are available, paid for by Christ. To extend the metaphor, Christ bought out the store, and all of God's supplies are now available freely to us. The Rock of Israel both protects us and supplies us.

CORNERSTONE

This leads us to a pivotal name of God from the Old Testament that prepares us for Jesus in the New. In Psalm 118:22, the psalmist first prophesies of Jesus as a particular kind of rock or stone, the cornerstone: "The stone that the builders rejected has become the cornerstone."

This verse in the original language says that the rejected stone has become the chief or corner of the structure being built. Jesus claimed this prophecy for himself in Matthew 21:42. Paul and Peter refer to Jesus as the cornerstone as well, not just the stone they rested on but the stone that set the foundation for all others.

Some translations use "keystone" or "capstone" in Psalm 118:22. While the cornerstone was foundational to the structure other stones were placed on, *capstone* denotes the crowning stone in a building or wall.[1] The capstone in an arch was called the keystone, the crowning piece that steadied the other stones and held the entire structure in place.

Why do I go into such detail about these types of stones? For me, visualizing this metaphor has steadied me in times of turmoil. In terms of the work to hold us fast and keep us until Christ's return, Fleming Rutledge says, that "God is the subject of the verb."[2] God is the active element from which all else flows. This is the promise offered through the cornerstone or keystone metaphor. Consider the role of the keystone in an arch. "A keystone (also known as capstone) is the wedge-shaped stone piece at the apex of a masonry arch or the generally round one at the apex of a vault. In both cases it is the final piece placed during construction and locks all the stones into position, allowing the arch or vault to bear weight."[3]

The keystone of an arch locks the other stones into position so that the arch can bear weight. The cornerstone of a building bears the weight of the rest of the structure as well. We sufferers are weight bearers, are we not? There is great pressure and responsibility on sufferers. We often carry the same responsibilities as others around us. We must still pay our bills. We must earn income. We must feed our children. We must fulfill our responsibilities at work or in our community. But we do so with heavy weights on us. We may have the extra weight of doctors' appointments and physical impairment. We have weights of sorrow and discouragement that drain us of energy. We have the weights of financial burdens and relational crises. We cannot bear these weights alone. Though others come alongside us to help, we will crumble under the weights on us without the Keystone that holds the arch together. "He is before all things, and by him all things hold together" (Colossians 1:17).

Jesus holds our faith together. Jesus holds our world together. And Jesus holds us together when we have lost control of our lives. "God is the subject of the verb."

> Therefore the Lord God said,
> Look, I have laid a stone in Zion,
> a tested stone,
> a precious cornerstone, a sure foundation;
> the one who believes will be unshakable. (Isaiah 28:16)

THE ROCK WHO RESTORES ZION

As I was writing this chapter, a dear brother in Christ whose family sat behind me most Sundays in church drowned during an otherwise peaceful outing with his wife. The pain of it for his wife and daughters, and our church family that loved him dearly, took my breath away. I carried a washcloth in my purse into his funeral service and warned my sons that I was going to cry a lot. I appreciated Henry and his kindness to our family, but my grief at that moment went beyond his unexpected death. One pastor sang an old song by Rich Mullins during the service that phrased it well, "If I weep let it be as a man who is longing for his home."[4]

I was embarrassed at my display of grief at Henry's funeral. But it was cumulative grief building up in me for years since I first realized I couldn't escape the death of my family unit. It was the grief of contemplating young mothers whose breast cancer was found at a much later stage than mine preparing their children for her death. It was the pain of watching my sons walking through fear and insecurity as their primary caregiver was unable to care for their most basic needs. And, now, it was the pain of contemplating Henry's wife, children, and grandchildren mourning the unexpected death of a man who had loved and provided for each well. He had been an example of Christ's love for the church to us all. The cumulative pain was too much.

When we have suffered in one area, I'm convinced we become more attuned to suffering in others. As painful as it is to grow in awareness of the depths of suffering in our world, we shouldn't be making our peace with the sin, suffering, and heartache in it. We should feel its cumulative effect as suffering outside us adds to the pain of the suffering inside us. This is natural. We were not created for divorce court, hospitals, or funeral homes. We should not make peace with them.

When my pastor got up to speak at Henry's funeral, he reminded us that we didn't have to put on a good show or speak positive

Christian buzz phrases at this moment. We could mourn. We could deeply grieve. Because God didn't create us for death. He didn't create us to be at peace with cancer, divorce, or unexpected drownings. He created humankind in Eden to enjoy relationship with him in an environment void of disease, death, or betrayal. It is unnatural to be content with this mess of a life because God created us for something much better.

We rightly mourn all that is wrong in the world, but we do not mourn without hope.

There are many encouraging passages in Scripture on God our Rock, but one has stood out to me above all others, stopping me in my tracks of pain and calling me to hope. It speaks to the deepest longings in my heart, the restoration of not just all that has been lost in my family and physical health, but all that has been lost in our world since Adam and Eve first sinned in the Garden of Eden.

> Listen to me, you who pursue righteousness,
> you who seek the LORD:
> Look to the rock from which you were cut,
> and to the quarry from which you were dug.
> Look to Abraham your father,
> and to Sarah who gave birth to you.
> When I called him, he was only one;
> I blessed him and made him many.
> For the LORD will comfort Zion;
> he will comfort all her waste places,
> and he will make her wilderness like Eden,
> and her desert like the garden of the LORD. (Isaiah 51:1-3)

The prophet Isaiah tells his listeners in verse 1, "Look to the rock from which you were cut." This Rock who is our foundation that catches us when we slip and fall is also our Source. He is the quarry from which we were dug, "the source and protector of our faith" (Hebrews 12:2).

Then Isaiah says in verse 2 to look to Abraham and Sarah. In the midst of comforting those in desolation, why would he turn the focus away from our supernatural God to these fallen humans? It was the very desolation of Abraham and Sarah's affliction of barrenness that highlighted the provision of Isaac in their old age. They lived with that affliction for decades, but they too were fruitful in the land of their affliction. They found laughter in their old age. They were unexpectedly fruitful when their circumstances and physical bodies said it was impossible. They named Isaac "laughter" not in spite of their age but because of their age and long history of barrenness. They recognized the provision of Isaac as a supernatural gift from God, and fruitfulness in that particular context gave them great joy.

Isaiah said all of this to a people whose land and lives lay in ruins around their feet. They felt the cumulative effects of the fall. Their land was a desert; their resources wasted. Look to this Rock, Isaiah told them. For he will comfort Zion. He will renew her like Eden, making her desert like the garden of the Lord.

Zion renewed. Eden restored. This is what we long for. This is what we need. Rich Mullins longed for it, weeping as a man who knew all was not right with the world, longing for his eternal home where there are no tears, hospitals, divorce courts, or funeral homes. God doesn't have to tell me to long for his kingdom to come. He didn't have to tell Mary or Martha to long for a time when their loved ones would never die. He didn't have to tell Job to desire a place where there was no disease or death. He didn't have to instruct Joseph to want the Promised Land. He didn't have to tell me, my boys, or Henry's family to long for the resurrection. Ultimately, Joseph, Mary, Martha, and Job naturally longed for Eden. We do too. We long for a place where death is nonexistent. Those longings were implanted in our DNA at creation.

> Oh, don't you want to go, to that gospel feast
> That promised land, that land where all is peace?
> Walk into heaven, and take a seat
> And cast my crown at Jesus' feet . . .
> Lord, I want to cross over into campground[5]

We long for Eden, but we are moving toward a land restored like Eden. We weep because we are longing for our home. But that home is approaching.

DESTROYERS THAT NO LONGER DESTROY

The first *Star Wars* movie ended with Luke Skywalker disabling and destroying the Death Star, which threatened the universe. *The Last Jedi* did similarly. Supremacy, the name of Emperor Snoke's latest star destroyer, was the loser this time. The Supremacy was the ultimate destroyer striking fear in the resistance as it tracked them through space, but it ended in disabled ruins, unable to harm the resistance any more. The Star Wars franchise has resonated with fans for decades because from the first episode released in 1977, it has told a version of the greatest story ever told, the destroyer destroyed, the annihilator of the universe disabled, exiled, and unable to permanently harm.

In the Star Wars franchise, Star Destroyers don't blow up stars and destroy entire planets nonstop. But when they aren't firing on planets, they are still threatening harm. The threat of destruction weighs on us as much as the actual blow when we sit in the shadow of a destroyer. One result of Henry's unexpected death in my life was the reminder that death can strike suddenly, in the midst of happy times. We sit in its shadow threatened by it even during seasons when our loved ones appear happy and safe.

Victory comes when the threat of destroyers is removed, when they are disabled and can no longer destroy. The disabled, crumbling destroyer is the first step toward freedom and restoration. At the end of *The Last Jedi*, the Resistance hadn't yet seen the full restoration of all that was lost under the emperor's oppressive regime, but with the threat of ultimate destruction removed, restoration had started nonetheless.

The prophet Isaiah, who exhorted us to look to the Rock, predicted the death of the ultimate destroyer in Isaiah 25:8.

> He will destroy death forever.
> The Lord GOD will wipe away the tears
> from every face
> and remove his people's disgrace
> from the whole earth,
> for the LORD has spoken.

Death is the great destroyer. Ultimately, it sits over us as the Supreme Death Star, threatening us and our loved ones with ultimate destruction. We at times cannot comprehend anything but utter destruction at its hands. But in 1 Corinthians 15:54-58, the apostle Paul wants us to know that Isaiah's prophecy has been fulfilled through Christ.

> **Death has been swallowed up in victory.**
> **Where, death, is your victory?**
> **Where, death, is your sting?**

The sting of death is sin, and the power of sin is the law. But thanks be to God, who gives us the victory through our Lord Jesus Christ!

Therefore, my dear brothers and sisters, be steadfast, immovable, always excelling in the Lord's work, because you know that your labor in the Lord is not in vain.

When Jesus paid for our sins and rose from the dead, he emasculated death, robbing it of its power over us. Hebrews 2:14 says that "through his death he [destroyed] the one holding the power of death—that is, the devil." As I sat at Henry's funeral weeping with longing for Eden, I was moved by the faithful praise of his wife and family, by friends at church who had known him much longer than I. Henry's loss struck them deeply, but neither they nor Henry were destroyed (2 Corinthians 4:9). Death doesn't have the last word over Henry or our church family.

After I found out I had breast cancer, another book sat staring at me from my bookshelf, Kara Tippetts's *The Hardest Peace*. Kara was diagnosed with late-stage breast cancer as she and her husband planted a church in Colorado while parenting four young children. Kara struggled in particular as she contemplated the pain for her young children of losing their mother. She reached out to her friend Blythe, who had lost both of her parents in a car accident in her youth. Kara needed to hear from another who had lost parents at a pivotal age that her children would be okay, that what seemed like a life destroyer wouldn't actually destroy her children.

Blythe responded to Kara with the reminders of God's grace that she needed. Blythe told Kara that God's grace toward her children would be breathtaking. What should have destroyed Blythe did not destroy her. What seemed destined to upend the lives of the Tippetts's children and destroy their hopes for the future would not actually destroy them either, Blythe assured Kara.[6] Death can still inflict pain, but it can no longer destroy us.

In light of death's emasculation, Paul exhorted believers in 1 Corinthians 15 to be *steadfast* and *immovable* in the work of the Lord because their labor wouldn't be in vain. Death could no longer destroy them or their legacy.

Steadfast.

Immovable.

You know what is steadfast and immovable? A rock.

> Look to the rock from which you were cut,
> and to the quarry from which you were dug. (Isaiah 51:1)

Do you see it now? Scripture brings us back full circle. Despite the weights on our backs and circumstances that threaten to destroy us, we can be steadfast and immovable in the work of Christ because we are rocks, dug from the quarry of the Rock of Israel himself. He is the cornerstone or keystone, the Rock we are founded on and the Rock pivotally positioned to bear the brunt of the weights on us. We are cut from the same quarry as him. Because he bears the center of the weight, we who are built on him, made from him, in union with him, have the necessary foundation to bear up under what would crush us without him.

The breaking of a covenant relationship would crush us without God our Rock. The physical death of a dearly loved one would destroy us without the Cornerstone holding us up. A medical diagnosis or financial loss that turns our life on its side would ruin us without the Rock of Israel shepherding us through it. These things knock us off our base into a pit without a foothold. But we were hewn from a bigger, firmer Rock, and he will lift us back up. What threatens to destroy us or our loved ones won't actually destroy us. The years the locust have eaten will be restored (Joel 2:25). Our wilderness will be made like Eden. Our desert will become a garden.

> For the LORD will comfort Zion;
> he will comfort all her waste places,
> and he will make her wilderness like Eden,
> and her desert like the garden of the LORD. (Isaiah 51:3)

This is our hope. Look to the Rock from which you were cut. He is leading us to a place described in Revelation 21:3-4 where "death will be no more." There, he will live with us and walk among us. Scripture tells us that he will "wipe away every tear from [our] eyes" (v. 4). When I read that, a sweet image forms in my mind of God's own gentle hand cradling our faces, one by one, wiping the tears from our cheeks with his thumb. Henry, his wife, and his daughters are all in line, followed by myself, my children, and a whole host of others. This Rock, who has stood strong under us, holding us up during the worst of life's griefs, is our gentle giant, our Father, our Savior, and our Friend. He is leading us to this place where "grief, crying, and pain will be no more" (v. 4). He will restore all that has been lost, making our deserts like the Garden of Eden he created us to happily enjoy with him.

REFLECT

Read Revelation 21:1-6. Can you envision your place in this scene with God your Father?

What pains in your life will have passed away?

How do you think you will feel internally as God wipes the tears from your eyes?

CONCLUSION

Limping Forward

As I recovered from each of my surgeries, I spent countless hours rocking in a chair on the screened porch of my farmhouse, staring at the land and fields. Again and again I would look past the towering oak in the center of my yard to see my dad limping from his little red office on our farm to the 1950s-era Quonset hut that holds his farm tools and whichever of his antique tractors he's trying to keep running at the time. Since his extended time in the ICU on a ventilator, he more often drives his truck from the office to the Quonset hut, but he still gets out of the truck, pushes the heavy doors to the hut open, and limps inside. Daddy is eighty-two years old and has congestive heart failure, poor circulation in his legs, and a painful hip that needs to be replaced. But he still gets up every day and limps forward.

Daddy is by no means the first Christian to persevere with either a literal or figurative limp. In Genesis 32:22-32, Jacob wrestled through the night with God himself. As daybreak approached, God dislocated Jacob's hip. But Jacob held on until God blessed him.

Jacob said, "I will not let you go unless you bless me."

"What is your name?" the man asked.

"Jacob," he replied.

"Your name will no longer be Jacob," he said. "It will be Israel because you have struggled with God and with men and have prevailed." . . .

And he blessed him there.

Jacob then named the place Peniel, "For I have seen God face to face," he said, "yet my life has been spared." The sun shone on him as he passed by Peniel—limping because of his hip. (Genesis 31:26-31)

Jacob walked forward blessed by God. With a limp. We don't know if he ever fully recovered from his dislocated hip. For however long he had it, this limp affected Jacob in serious ways. His family was dependent on him, and he himself was dependent on his legs for travel. The paradox of a blessed life marred by a bone out of joint was real for Jacob, and it is real for us.

Like Jacob, I walk forward in life with a limp. At times I feel like I experienced an amputation. My divorce cut off my one-flesh relationship with another, and I continue to feel this loss in acute ways daily. I also experienced a true physical amputation when I had my mastectomy. The scars across my torso daily remind me of emotional, relational, and physical loss I've experienced. And the pain in my hands and feet remind me of the chronic illnesses I will likely endure until I die. Many believers whose stories were preserved in Scripture for us, and even more who have lived in the centuries since, have walked forward with a limp, with permanent scars from their own journey of suffering. Limping believers can still be blessed. And like Jacob, the blessing is often wrapped up in the very same set of circumstances that caused our limp. It is a true paradox.

CARRY THAT CROSS

In chapter two of this book we were presented with Jesus' words to his disciples: "If anyone wants to follow after me, let him deny himself, take up his cross daily, and follow me" (Luke 9:23). These crosses Jesus instructs us to take up are the very things that cause us to limp. They are the weights on our back that threaten to push our face into the ground—that lost relationship, that terrible medical diagnosis, that debilitating financial setback. At times we feel crushed by their weight, pressed into the dirt, unable to get to our feet. But Paul reminded believers in Corinth that though they were afflicted with great burdens, they weren't actually crushed (2 Corinthians 4: 8). What presses us down will not destroy us because Christ bears the weights with and for us. Adjust the weights on your shoulders, Jesus exhorted his disciples, and limp forward after him anyway. The Keystone carries the greatest of the weight so we may bear up under it.

Since the day it dawned on me I couldn't rescue my family from divorce, I prayed each New Year and birthday that this would be the year things turned around for me and my children. I have longed for financial stability, physical health, and spiritual purpose. But every year, stability instead seemed further out of reach.

This year I woke up on the morning of my forty-eighth birthday to the realization that something had shifted in my head from previous years of hope for a better year. It felt a bit like the one time I rode a cantering horse that shifted into a full gallop. Galloping was exhilaratingly smooth compared to the trot. For me this mental transition was from the bumpy, stressful resistance to suffering I had felt for years to an acceptance of my circumstances with eternal hope. I stopped praying for relief from my struggles and instead asked to lean closer into Christ so I could persevere with hope as I struggled, taking hold of him as he has hold of me. I prayed for God's help to adjust the burdens on my back. I prayed he'd help me carry these burdens and follow him anyway.

Sara Groves sings of this transition in her beautiful song "Less Like Scars":

> Less like a prison, more like my room
> It's less like a casket, more like a womb . . .
> And in your hands the pain and hurt
> Look less like scars and more like character.[1]

As Sara sings, I too have found my journey less like a prison, more like a room, less like a casket, more like a womb.

The cloud of witnesses testify to us too that scars fade over time, and in their place we see we are conformed to the image of Christ, his character forged in our heart and soul as a result of our hard journey. The fellowship of suffering has begun its perfect work in my life. Hope dawns for my future, not in earthly prosperity but in confidence of the Rock who is higher than I, my firm foundation as I walk forward in faith. Like Jesus, for the joy set before us beckoning across the great divide, we can endure our cross and the shame some might project on us with an eye on Jesus in his throne room, where he sits with both authority and compassion.

Our brothers and sisters in Christ among us who have suffered, the cloud of witnesses in heaven, Job, David, Asaph, Rahab, and even Jesus himself, all point you and me in our darkest days to their hope. It didn't disappoint them, and it won't disappoint us. Though we may limp to the bitter end of life, we can confidently believe that when we see Jesus face-to-face for the first time in heaven, we won't be disappointed by the outcome of our lives. May that hope, reinforced by those who have shared with us during our afflictions, sustain us as we limp forward until the day our faith becomes sight.

I know how to get along with humble means, and I also know how to live in prosperity; in any and every circumstance I have learned the secret of being filled and going hungry, both of having abundance and suffering need. I can do all things through Him who strengthens me. Nevertheless, you have done well to share *with me* in my affliction. (Philippians 4:12-14 NASB)

ACKNOWLEDGMENTS

Though I have often felt alone, it is not the fault of those who have loved me well and walked closely beside me. Thank you to Mama, Daddy, Karey, Donna, Dupre, and Joey. To JP and Laurie, John Mark and Shea. To Christine, Karen, Jonna, Bina, Denie, Marcia, Kitty, Claire, Rachael, Bekah, Hannah, and dearest Randall.

To Jen.

To Ted and Sarah, Dennis and Krista, John and Linn, and Matt and Edna. To Nate and Greg. To Amy. To Jeanne.

To Lee Ann and Kerri. To Mary Beth and Wanda. To Lisa and Susan. To Karen. To Cheryl.

To Melanie, who insisted on being my companion at the hospital before I knew how much I would need one.

And to Tiffany, the gift from God that I tried to push away. Instead, God insisted you live with us, and I've thanked him ever since. I literally wouldn't have survived that dark season without you.

God has been kind to me through you all.

APPENDIX

Offering Companionship to the Suffering

How can we help a suffering friend or family member in practical ways? There tend to be two circles of need—acute, in-house need supplied by closest friends and family, and the second level of support that bolsters the first.

In times of acute, in-house need, your suffering loved one may feel numbed, barely able to function. Even in this state of acute grief, numbness, or physical pain, remember to keep your suffering loved one informed and included in what is happening. After my worst surgery, I remember my sister telling me during my first days back home what she was doing and why she was doing it. Then she'd make sure that was okay with me. Most of the time I was high on pain meds, struggling to move at all, and going to dark places when I did think due to cancer in my lymph node. But I did have occasional opinions, things that were important to me. Her method of handling food and my physical care in those first days was a lesson to me I hope I can use when walking with others in future situations of deep pain or struggle.

As time goes on, remember that grief looks and feels different for everyone. Grief, even the acute early stages, doesn't have a specified time frame. Furthermore, the fact that someone seems better one day—or week or month—doesn't mean they are past their grief. Grief ebbs and flows like waves on a beach. One friend recounted to me the frustration of this ebb and flow of grief for her family. After times of deep sorrow she grasped to find the good. She wanted to emerge from the dark. But friends and family expected a linear progression to her grief. They seemed surprised (and sometimes offended) when she laughed or found happiness before they thought appropriate. They also seemed surprised when she would descend again into dark thoughts and emotions. Grief doesn't fit a tidy chart of stages. If you are walking with someone on a long journey of suffering, allow them unexpected times of joy or happiness. Afterward, don't be surprised if they descend again into grief.

For those supporting a sufferer for the long haul, whether you are in the first or second level of support, remember this important truth. General concern for or good will toward a sufferer is not the same as true compassion. A desire to help someone is not the same thing as actually helping that person! You cannot be helpful to a sufferer without recognizing the difference in these two. *Compassion* comes from the Latin for entering into the suffering of another. It is not waving from the outside of the tent of suffering with a concerned look on your face. Compassion enters the tent of suffering. It sits with the sufferer and feels the weight of suffering with them.

PRACTICAL COMPASSION

Those undergoing long-term trials and weights of suffering need many different friends and family to enter their suffering in ways that are truly helpful to the sufferer. No one person can help in all the ways a sufferer might need, but we are gifted in various ways in the body of Christ to come alongside another as we can. I have not done a very good job of walking with others through their own struggles in the past. I have often desired to help, but I have also settled for things that satisfied my desire to be seen as caring while not being tangibly helpful to the friend or family member who was suffering. Through my own recent journey, I have learned a few particularly important practical things that I hope will be helpful to others.

1. *Allow for lament.* Often I have been tempted to shut down conversations with someone who is grieving by giving them solutions or advice. I didn't understand, until I needed to do it myself, a sufferer's need to sit in lament. Lament isn't comfortable. The physical accoutrements of sackcloths and ashes in the Old Testament give testimony to the uncomfortable nature of lament. Many of us respond to unresolved discomfort by naturally trying to comfort. But the process of grief and lament is necessary to get to true comfort. If we interrupt the painful process early because we are uncomfortable sitting with a friend in their lament, we act like a doctor who sews up an abscessed surgical site before thoroughly cleaning it.

I have sweet friends who have endured with me over and over again as I lamented. As I've mentioned before, most of them had lamented their own deep suffering before walking with me through mine. They recognized my need to lament my own trials when I couldn't put words to them myself. Lament can be nonverbal. We can feel so low that we cannot put words to our pain. This is a reasonable response, one we are taught in Romans 8:26 that the Holy Spirit walks through with us. But lament can be loud and angry as well. My lament has taken the form of both frustrated verbal processing and morosely staring out the window. Both forms are uncomfortable for others, but they are a necessary part of the journey. It is a great grace to your suffering loved one when you affirm that what they mourn is worth mourning and sit with them as they do so.

2. *Insist on specific ways to help.* I sit today recovering from surgery number five in fifteen months. In tears. It happens every single time. I've learned that the path to surgery, the recovery after it, and the rhythm of ongoing doctors' appointments inevitably involve tears and frustrations. For single parents the path is particularly fraught with frustration because you don't have another adult in the house day in and day out who can help you process what you and your family need. Many days I couldn't think through what I needed from others, emotionally or physically. Still today I often can't think through the questions I need to ask doctors. I can't think through what I need from the grocery store. I can't think through what my kids will need to eat on a given day. I have benefitted from family and friends who have insisted on being with me.

In the early days of my diagnosis my cousin, a physical therapist, would not take no for an answer. At first I was annoyed and embarrassed. I still thought I was strong enough to navigate things, and I didn't want to put her out again and again. But she persisted, going with me to multiple doctors' appointments in different cities and was the deep help to me I didn't yet know I needed. Cousin Melanie knew what I needed before I did. You know why Melanie knew? Because she had been through a similar surgery herself and had walked with another family member through a cancer diagnosis just a year before. She was enabled to help me through her own previous experiences. She insisted on going with me to crucial doctors' appointments. And she insisted on spending the first night with me in the hospital after my first two major surgeries. I woke up in the ICU after my mastectomy to Melanie offering me lip balm, a modern version of the cup of cold water Jesus speaks of in Matthew 10.

My sister also insisted on staying with me after two of my surgeries. She too had been through her own painful surgery requiring months of recuperation. And she knew better than I what I would need after mine. It was a cup of cold water to me when I thought I would die of thirst. Not everyone is gifted to sit with someone in their hospital room. But if you are, offer to do that specifically with your loved one. Offer, even insist, to go with them to the doctor, to take them early in the morning to their procedure as my other sister did, to sit in the waiting room and hear from the doctor when other family members cannot, as a friend from church did, and to stay with them the first night after surgery as Cousin Melanie did twice. I had family and friends willing to do this with me, often insisting when I didn't think I needed it, and their practical compassion blessed me deeply.

My church family offered specific help again and again, help that I initially resisted, to be honest, out of pride. They provided meals before surgeries and after, again and again. Women came together to pay for a house cleaner for six weeks after one surgery. Oh, what a help that was. And in an especially sweet gesture, two elders' wives cleaned out my pantry. These practical helps that brought order back to my home helped bring order back to my mind as well.

3. Few sufferers are going to let you know if they need something. I don't know why the statement "Let me know if you need something" persists in our vocabulary. Most people know deep down how unhelpful it is. As someone who has personally used it herself in good will toward many others, I acknowledge that people use it with a sincere desire to be helpful. But the desire to be helpful is not the same as actually being helpful. And sometimes the desire to be viewed as compassionate and helpful actually hides personal insecurity. The open offer to help, untied to a specific thing that would require your own personal thought or sacrifice, can make us feel good about ourselves, but it does nothing for the one suffering who likely can't think through what they need. It functions as our "get out of jail free" card. When a sufferer is in crisis, you can feel vindicated that if they had only let you know, you could have helped them avoid it. Your conscience is salved.

The problem is that helping a sufferer isn't about our personal conscience. It's not about us feeling like we have been a good friend, done our duty, or performed the required sacrificial Christian service. Helping a sufferer is simply about, well, helping the sufferer. If you attach to your help some good feeling of doing your duty, I can guarantee you will not actually be helpful to a sufferer. Because you will also inevitably attach to it your bad feelings when you are not able to do what they need. And that is an unfair emotional burden to place on someone who is struggling. I've had a few situations when someone tried to help me out of duty or to feel good about themselves. I've had many others when I tried to help someone else out of that sense for myself. I'll be frank. That is a sinful foundation on which to try to minister to another, and it puts an unbearable weight on the sufferer.

If you want to help someone because you love them and don't want them to carry the weight by themselves, then figure out the specific ways you can help them. If, in contrast, you offer help out of guilt, you will inevitably make the person you are helping feel guilty for bothering you.

What can you practically offer that would be helpful to a suffering friend? Perhaps you can offer to receive a text, night or day, with an emergency emotional need. This is especially effective if you are an out-of-town friend who literally cannot help in person. I am so thankful for the friends I can text or email "I don't think I'm going to make it." I have truly felt when friends pray for me. God works in some way every time, most often in my own mental state.

If you live far away, you can still contribute a meal. I have sent pizza to many friends on the opposite coast through delivery meal apps like Grubhub. Whether you live close or far away, you can offer to pay a house cleaner. I have found it hard to allow someone else to clean my house. Nevertheless, my house needs cleaning, and I often cannot do it myself. My mother and friends from church have both paid for a house cleaner to come, and it has blessed me greatly. My mom also often comes midweek to clean my kitchen and wash a load of clothes. It doesn't take her long, and my house still has a lot of needs. But that one gesture helps me mentally very much. My mom can't do everything, but she does the thing she can.

Several friends and family have taken my boys to fun activities. This has meant the world to me. I lament that their childhood has been marred by the dismemberment of our family unit and my ongoing health struggles. I long to make up for those losses with fun experiences. When I can't, our larger church and family community have come together to make sure my boys make it to church camp, the latest Star Wars movie, or the 4-D *Polar Express* experience at our state museum.

There is a multitude of practical ways to help a sufferer. It is work sometimes to figure out exactly how your giftings fit into the multiple moving parts that make up their needs. I for one am not a stellar cook. It pains me to admit it, but I have learned I am more likely to bless a friend by offering to pick up pizza for them or take them to a doctor's appointment than I am to cook them a homemade meal. It will bless you and your loved one to figure out the best way you can step into their tent with help they need.

4. It's not the sufferer's job to keep you informed. If you want to know what's going on in the progression of a disease, the downfall of a marriage, or the resolution of a court case, do not rely on the one most closely affected to remember to tell you. They are weary, and they are trying their best to keep their own head above the water. A friend told me of receiving the results of blood work that confirmed she was miscarrying her first child. She sat in numbed silence in the same seat for some period of time after receiving the call. Her grandmother happened to call to tell her she was praying for her, and my friend told her the sad results she had just received. The grandmother called her daughter, my friend's mother, to tell her. Her mother then emailed my friend, "That was a terrible way for me to find out!" This all happened within a few hours of my friend learning that she was losing her baby.

Another friend had a similar situation when she received news of a last-minute court date for a painful trial proceeding after the murder of her brother. Another when her recovery took a turn for the worse three weeks after surgery. Extended family and friends acted like they were the offended parties for not knowing of these turns. Unexpected turns in a long path of suffering should be, well, expected. It is not the job of the one suffering the most deeply to keep others informed. They often are simply incapable of having the emotionally draining conversations again and again or thinking through the logistics of who they need to inform when they are struggling deeply themselves.

The errors of those interactions are clear to any of us emotionally distant from the circumstances. But when you love someone going through such an event, and you hurt as well when they get unexpected bad news, it is hard not to take offense when they do not inform you as often or in the way you think appropriate. I have learned that if I want to stay informed about the suffering of another, then it is my responsibility to ask. I now try to put a reminder in my calendar to check in with friends or family in long-term situations of struggle. And if I do find out after the fact of a crucial surgery, court proceeding, or other turn of events, I recognize now that it is not the sufferer's fault I wasn't informed.

5. Give and receive grace for yourself and your suffering friend. The bottom line of walking with a suffering loved one is that none of us can walk the road of suffering flawlessly. None suffer perfectly, and none of us who come alongside as their companions will either. The tent of suffering is a horrible place to try to feel good about yourself. If you are insecure or needy or feel constant guilt because of your shortcomings, you need to remove yourself from the tent for a bit and understand Christ's payment for your sins and inadequacies. Jesus covers your guilt, and there is no condemnation for those in Christ Jesus (Romans 8:1). This gospel truth allows you to walk the road of suffering with another without shame when balls get dropped. You can confess and repair your relationship with your loved one. Your mistakes or outright sins don't define you. Understand this truth from the good news of Jesus Christ, and then reenter the tent with your suffering loved one with practical compassion.

NOTES

1 ON THE OUTSIDE LOOKING IN

[1]"Pariah," *Encyclopaedia Britannica*, accessed August 19, 2019, www.britannica
.com/topic/pariah.

2 OUR SUFFERING SAVIOR

[1]"*Yada'*," *Bible Study Tools*, accessed August 19, 2019, www.biblestudytools.com
/lexicons/hebrew/nas/yada.html.

[2]"*Sympatheō*," *Bible Study Tools*, accessed August 19, 2019, www.biblestudytools
.com/lexicons/greek/nas/sumpatheo.html.

[3]"*Koinōnia*," *Bible Study Tools*, accessed August 19, 2019, www.biblestudytools.com
/lexicons/greek/nas/koinonia.html.

[4]Some material in this section and in other chapters (3 percent of the content from
this point forward) is adapted from reflections I originally recounted on my blog,
Practical Theology for Women, https://theologyforwomen.org.

3 FELLOWSHIP OF THE SUFFERING

[1]Kate Snow, "Loneliness Can Be Hazardous to Your Health, Experts Warn,"
Today, April 23, 2018, www.today.com/health/how-stop-feeling-lonely-social
-media-can-worsen-loneliness-t127466.

[2]"*Parakaleō*," *Bible Study Tools*, accessed August 20, 2019, www.biblestudytools
.com/lexicons/greek/kjv/parakaleo.html.

[3]Dee Brestin, *The God of All Comfort* (Grand Rapids: Zondervan, 2015), 161.

[4]Brestin, *God of All Comfort*, 160-61.

4 PLEADING FOR RESCUE

[1]"*Ratson*," *The Hebrew-Greek Keyword Study Bible*, ed. Spiros Zodhiates (Chattanooga,
TN: AMG Publishers, 2018), 2029.

[2]"*Ratson*," *Keyword Study Bible*, 2029.

5 HELP MY UNBELIEF

[1]J. I. Packer explores these attributes of God in depth in *Knowing God* (Downers
Grove, IL: InterVarsity Press, 1993).

[2]Charlie Dates, (@CharlieDates), "There is a kind of danger in power, a bit of slavery in wealth, and a latent misfortune in comfort. There must be, has to be real joy found somewhere else," Twitter, May 24, 2018, 7:27 a.m., https://twitter.com/CharlieDates/status/999658119499313152.

6 AMBIGUOUS LOSS

[1]Names have been changed to protect the privacy of these individuals.

[2]"Ambiguous Loss: Grief, Loss, and Depression," Seattle Christian Counseling, October 30, 2015, https://seattlechristiancounseling.com/articles/ambiguous-loss-grief-loss-and-depression-2.

[3]Lamentations traditionally has been attributed to Jeremiah, though some scholars question the authorship of the book.

[4]C. S. Lewis, *The Last Battle*, The Chronicles of Narnia (New York: Harper Collins, 2002), 228.

9 WAITING ON JESUS

[1]"*Thorybeō*," *Bible Study Tools*, accessed August 22, 2019, www.biblestudytools.com/lexicons/greek/nas/thorubeo.html.

[2]"*Meris*," *Bible Study Tools*, accessed August 22, 2019, www.biblestudytools.com/lexicons/greek/nas/meris.html.

[3]"Four Temperaments," *Wikipedia*, accessed August 22, 2019, https://en.wikipedia.org/wiki/Four_temperaments.

[4]Andrew Wilson and Rachel Wilson, *The Life We Never Expected: Hopeful Reflections on the Challenges of Parenting Children with Special Needs* (Wheaton, IL: Crossway, 2016), 80-81.

10 FELLOWSHIP WITH THE CLOUD OF WITNESSES

[1]Elisabeth Elliot, *These Strange Ashes* (Grand Rapids: Revell, 1998), 147.

[2]Author unknown, "A Little Talk with Jesus," *NegroSpirituals.com*, accessed August 23, 2019, www.negrospirituals.com/songs/a_little_talk_with_jesus.htm.

[3]From Sara Groves reworking of one of the most famous spirituals of all. Sara Groves, "When the Saints," promotional single, INO Records, 2007.

[4]Robert Patrick, "Faria Verdict Leaves Many Questions Unanswered About Lincoln County Murder," *St. Louis Post-Dispatch*, November 8, 2015, www.stltoday.com/news/local/crime-and-courts/faria-verdict-leaves-many-questions-unanswered-about-lincoln-county-murder/article_bb8f6665-47b3-5068-95de-97a902daf367.html.

[5]"Witness," *Merriam-Webster*, accessed August 23, 2019, www.merriam-webster.com/dictionary/witness.

[6]"*Archēgos*," *Bible Study Tools*, accessed August 23, 2019, www.biblestudytools.com/lexicons/greek/nas/archegos.html; "*Archē*," *Bible Study Tools*, accessed August 23, 2019, www.biblestudytools.com/lexicons/greek/nas/arche.html; and "*Agō*," *Bible Study Tools*, accessed August 23, 2019, www.biblestudytools.com/lexicons/greek/nas/ago.html.

11 FELLOWSHIP WITH THE ROCK

[1]"Capstone," *Bible Study Tools*, accessed August 23, 2019, www.biblestudytools.com/dictionaries/bakers-evangelical-dictionary/capstone.html.

[2]Fleming Rutledge, *Advent: The Once and Future Coming of Jesus Christ* (Grand Rapids: Eerdmans, 2018), chap. 7, Kindle.

[3]"Keystone," *Wikipedia*, accessed August 23, 2019, https://en.wikipedia.org/wiki/Keystone (architecture).

[4]Rich Mullins and Steve Cudworth, "If I Stand," *Songs*, Brentwood, TN: Reunion Records, 1996.

[5]"Deep River," *NegroSpirituals.com*, accessed August 26, 2019, www.negrospirituals.com/songs/deep_river.htm.

[6]Kara Tippetts, *The Hardest Peace: Expecting Grace in the Midst of Life's Hard* (Colorado Springs, CO: David C. Cook, 2014), 138.

CONCLUSION: LIMPING FORWARD

[1]Sara Groves, "Less Like Scars," *All Right Here*, Brentwood, TN: INO Records, 2002.

SUGGESTED READING

KEY SCRIPTURE
Psalm 88; 137; 143
Isaiah 26:3
Isaiah 53
The Gospel of Luke
Romans 8
1 Corinthians 12
Ephesians 1:15-23
Colossians 1:9-20
Hebrews 11–12

BOOKS
Brestin, Dee. *God of All Comfort*. Grand Rapids: Zondervan, 2015.
Elliot, Elisabeth. *A Chance to Die*. Grand Rapids: Revell, 1987.
Elliot, Elisabeth. *These Strange Ashes*. Grand Rapids: Revell, 1998.
Guthrie, Nancy. *Hearing Jesus Speak into Your Sorrow*. Wheaton, IL: Tyndale Momentum, 2009.
Hill, Wesley. *Washed and Waiting*. Grand Rapids: Zondervan, 2016.
Keller, Tim. *Walking with God Through Pain and Suffering*. New York: Penguin, 2015.
Lewis, C. S. *The Last Battle*. The Chronicles of Narnia. New York: Harper Collins, 2002.
Newbell, Trillia J. *Sacred Endurance*. InterVarsity Press, 2019.
Packer, J. I. *Knowing God*. Downers Grove, IL: InterVarsity Press, 1993.
Reissig, Courtney. *Teach Me to Feel*. The Good Book Company, 2020.
Rowe, Sheila Wise. *Healing Racial Trauma*. InterVarsity Press, 2020.
Sojourner Truth. *The Narrative of Sojourner Truth*. New York: Penguin, 1998.
Ten Boom, Corrie. *The Hiding Place*. Grand Rapids: Chosen Books, 2006.
Wilson, Andrew, and Rachel Wilson. *The Life We Never Expected: Hopeful Reflections on the Challenges of Parenting Children with Special Needs*. Wheaton, IL: Crossway, 2016.

SCRIPTURE INDEX

OLD TESTAMENT

Genesis
3:15, *130*
31:26-31, *156*
32:22-32, *155*
37–50, *75, 132*
41:52, *133*
43:30, *75*
45:1-2, *75*
49, *140*
49:22-24, *141*
49:25, *141*

Exodus
16, *78*

Numbers
14, *77*

Deuteronomy
32:4, *142*

Joshua
2, *138*
2:8-13, *138*

2 Samuel
15:30, *75*

Job
1:1-12, *98*
2:11, *98*
3:20-21, *91*
3:20-26, *98*
3:25-26, *91*
7, *94*
7:1-4, *93*

7:7, *93*
7:11, *93*
7:20, *94*
8, *113*
9, *94*
9:1, *96*
9:22, *94*
9:32, *96*
9:33, *96*
10:20-22, *95*
19:25-27, *97*
38, *93*
38:1-7, *102*
38:31-35, *103*
42, *108*
42:2-6, *106*
42:7, *113*
42:7-8, *92, 109*

Psalms
1, *43*
18, *143*
18:2, *142*
23, *43*
51, *43*
69, *42, 43, 44, 45, 47, 52,*
   54, 55, 58, 60
69:1-4, *44*
69:4, *51*
69:13-18, *48*
69:21, *53*
69:32-36, *54*
73, *43, 57, 61, 62, 65, 67,*
   70, 93, 95, 112, 117, 143
73:1-2, *57*
73:1-16, *71*
73:3-5, *58*
73:6-8, *59*

73:9-11, *59*
73:12-15, *60*
73:16-17, *62*
73:18-20, *64*
73:21-22, *66*
73:23-24, *67*
73:25-26, *69*
73:27-28, *71*
118:22, *144*
119, *43*
130:3, *96*
136, *64*
150, *43*

Proverbs
1:7, *106, 107*
3:5-6, *76*

Ecclesiastes
4:9-10, *38*

Isaiah
25:8, *150*
26:3, *17*
28:16, *145*
49, *49, 50*
49:8-9, *50*
51:1, *152*
51:1-3, *147*
51:3, *153*
53, *12*
53:3, *124*
53:4, *14*
53:5, *24*

Jeremiah
30:10, *83*
30:17, *83*

31:4, *83*
31:4-5, *83*

Lamentations
3:9, *76*

Joel
2:25, *153*

NEW TESTAMENT

Matthew
10:38-39, *11*
11:28-30, *21*
12:20, *46*
20:28, *18*
21:42, *144*
26:26, *81*
27:51, *63*

Mark
2, *37*
10:45, *53*

Luke
9, *11, 14*
9:23, *11, 157*
10, *117*
10:38-42, *115*
14, *11*

John
6, *36, 78*
6:32-35, *79*
6:68, *36*
11, *115, 117, 118*
11:4-6, *119*
11:5-6, *125*
11:6, *120*
11:32, *122*
11:32-35, *119*
11:35, *9*
12:24, *134*
14, *8, 31*
14:16, *8*
14:18, *8, 13*
15:5, *14, 24, 84*

15:15, *18*
15:16, *134*

Acts
2, *17*
2:42, *17, 31*

Romans
1:16, *52*
5:1-5, *52*
8:1, *50, 67*
8:26, *13*
9:33, *39*
10:9-10, *50*

1 Corinthians
12:12-14, *35*
12:26, *35*
15:54-58, *150*

2 Corinthians
1, *31*
1:3-5, *28*
1:4, *30, 33*
4, *157*
4:9, *151*
5:7, *129*
5:21, *67*
6:2, *50, 55*
7:4, *17*
9:8, *69*
10:5, *23*

Ephesians
1, *20, 68*
1:2, *68*
1:3, *68*
1:14, *14*
2:13, *53*
2:19, *97*
5:23, *14*
6:10, *140*
6:16-17, *143*

Philippians
1:5, *18*
3, *34*
3:8, *39*

3:10, *15, 17, 123*
3:10-12, *24*
4:12-14, *159*

Colossians
1:13, *53*
1:17, *145*
2:6-7, *14*

2 Timothy
2:24-26, *65*

Titus
2:14, *53*

Hebrews
2, *53*
2:8, *53, 55, 131*
2:14, *151*
2:18, *14*
4:12, *43*
4:15, *13*
4:16, *63, 64, 70, 72*
5:12, *129*
10:19-22, *63*
10:23, *136*
10:25, *129*
10:38, *113*
11, *131, 132*
11–12, *137*
11:1, *129*
11:4-5, *130*
11:6, *129*
11:7, *130*
11:11, *131*
11:21, *131*
11:22, *132*
11:39-40, *134, 137*
12:1, *135*
12:2, *16, 148*

1 Peter
4:13, *123*

Revelation
21:1-6, *153*
21:3-4, *153*